Best Easy Day Hikes
Lake Tahoe

Help Us Keep This Guide Up to Date

Every effort has been made by the author and editors to make this guide as accurate and useful as possible. However, many things can change after a guide is published—trails are rerouted, regulations change, techniques evolve, facilities come under new management, etc.

We would appreciate hearing from you concerning your experiences with this guide and how you feel it could be improved and kept up to date. While we may not be able to respond to all comments and suggestions, we'll take them to heart, and we'll also make certain to share them with the author. Please send your comments and suggestions to the following address:

Globe Pequot
Reader Response/Editorial Department
246 Goose Lane
Guilford, CT 06437

Or you may e-mail us at: editorial@falcon.com

Thanks for your input, and happy trails!

Best Easy Day Hikes Series

Best Easy Day Hikes
Lake Tahoe

Fourth Edition

Tracy Salcedo

FALCONGUIDES

GUILFORD, CONNECTICUT
HELENA, MONTANA

FALCONGUIDES®

An imprint of The Rowman & Littlefield Publishing Group, Inc.
4501 Forbes Blvd., Ste. 200
Lanham, MD 20706
www.rowman.com
Falcon and FalconGuides are registered trademarks and Make Adventure Your Story is a trademark of The Rowman & Littlefield Publishing Group, Inc.

Distributed by NATIONAL BOOK NETWORK

Maps by Melissa Baker

British Library Cataloguing-in-Publication Information Available

Library of Congress Cataloging-in-Publication Data
Names: Salcedo, Tracy, author.
Title: Best easy day hikes, Lake Tahoe / Tracy Salcedo.
Description: Fourth Edition. | Guilford, Connecticut : FalconGuides, [2019]
| Series: Best Easy Day Hikes series | "Distributed by NATIONAL BOOK
NETWORK"—T.p. verso. | "Previous editions of this book were published by
Falcon Publishing, Inc. in 1999, 2010, and 2015" —T.p. verso. |
Identifiers: LCCN 2018054308 (print) | LCCN 2018056303 (ebook)
| ISBN 9781493041107 (Electronic) | ISBN 9781493041091 |
ISBN 9781493041091¬q(hardcover/paperback : alk. paper) | ISBN
9781493041107¬q(e-book)
Subjects: LCSH: Hiking—Tahoe, Lake, Region (Calif. and Nev.)—Guidebooks.
| Walking—Tahoe, Lake, Region (Calif. and Nev.)—Guidebooks. |
Mountaineering—Tahoe, Lake, Region (Calif. and Nev.)—Guidebooks. |
Backpacking—Tahoe, Lake, Region (Calif. and Nev.)—Guidebooks. | Trails—
Tahoe, Lake, Region (Calif. and Nev.)—Guidebooks. | Tahoe, Lake, Region
(Calif. and Nev.)—Guidebooks.
Classification: LCC GV199.42.T16 (ebook) | LCC GV199.42.T16 S35 2019
(print) | DDC 917.94/38—dc23
LC record available at https://lccn.loc.gov/2018054308

Once and always, for the Friedman and Rodman families

Contents

Kilometers

Miles

N

Mount Rose

To
Reno

Truckee

Martis Creek
Lake

MOUNT ROSE
WILDERNESS

CALIFORNIA

Tahoe Vista

Incline Village

Carnelian Bay

Kings
Beach

Crystal
Bay

LAKE
TAHOE-
NEVADA
STATE
PARK

Marlette Lake

Tahoe City

Lake
Tahoe

Tahoe Pines

Spooner
Lake

To
Carson
City

Homewood

Glenbrook

Tahoma

SUGAR PINE
POINT
STATE PARK

Meeks Bay

NEVADA

Zephyr
Cove

D. L. BLISS
STATE PARK

EMERALD BAY
STATE PARK

Stateline

DESOLATION
WILDERNESS

Cascade Lake

South
Lake
Tahoe

Fallen Leaf
Lake

Lake Aloha

CALIFORNIA

Echo Lakes

To Sacramento

Acknowledgments

Thanks to the following folks for their advice and help with previous editions of this guide: Mike St. Michel, Lindsay Gusses, Garrett Villanueva, and Don Lane of the US Forest Service Lake Tahoe Basin Management Unit; Dave Nettle of Alpenglow Sports; Gisela Steiner of Tahoe Trail Trekkers; Mark Kimbrough and Morgan Fessler of the Tahoe Rim Trail Association; Hal Paris and Pandora Bahlman of the Incline Village General Improvement District; Roger Adamson, park superintendent of the Tahoe City Public Utility District; Scott Elliott of the California State Parks, Sierra State Parks Foundation; Bill Houdyschell of the forestry division of the Tahoe Donner Association; Bill Champion of Lake Tahoe–Nevada State Park; Dean Lutz, Jeff Wiley, and Susanne Jensen of Tahoe National Forest; and Jacqui Zink, park ranger with the US Army Corps of Engineers at Martis Creek Lake; Bill Schneider; editors David Lee, Charlene Patterson, Erica Olsen, and David Legere at FalconGuides.

Thanks to these folks for everything: the Friedman and Rodman clans; the Salcedo clan; the Chourré clan; Julie Roth and Oliver Aslin, Caitlin Brown, and my sons, Cruz, Jesse, and Penn.

Introduction

When I pulled together the first edition of this little guide, my youngest son accompanied me on many of these hikes. His contentment helped define my "best easy" baseline: If I could carry him without getting too winded, and if we were out and back before he got irritable, and if I liked what I saw along the way, we had a winner. We ambled through the woods together and I taught him his colors: green for the needles and leaves on the trees, brown for the bark and the dirt underfoot, blue for the sky and the lake and the pack he rode in. I'd ask the question: "What color is the water?" "Black," he would respond. He was 2, after all.

Now he's 22, and he's got the color thing all figured out. And me? Well, easy hikes are still the best, in my view. A well-maintained treadway; 6 miles round-trip, tops; great views and maybe a summit or a waterfall along the way; and back at the car, the beach, or the coffee shop before I get irritable . . . there's no better way to spend a day in the Lake Tahoe area. From shoreline to rim, whether tramping through a wildflower meadow or escaping to the lakeside to slip hot feet into the cold blue lake, Tahoe welcomes. Adventurer, wanderer, seeker, romantic, student, environmentalist, lazy slug who wants no more than a warm slab of granite on which to recline—Tahoe is the place to be.

The twenty-nine easy day hikes described in this edition include favorites that never lose their appeal, a pair of fun additions, and brief reprises of trails that didn't make the cut for lack of space. The routes are intended to showcase the various facets of Lake Tahoe and its environs, from lakeside to ridgeline, forest to meadow.

Selecting the "best" day hikes continues to present a pleasant conundrum—the options are numerous, and there's not a dud in the bunch. The trick has been to pick hikes that satisfy the intrepid visitor and curious resident alike. These hikes range from wheelchair-accessible interpretive trails to mildly taxing treks to high-altitude viewpoints. Some routes are ideal for adventure, some for contemplation, some for a Sunday afternoon outing with the family, and others for winding down on a summer evening after a hard day's work.

I hope this little labor of love inspires you to hike farther and more often. Onward and upward.

Tahoe in Brief

People have been drawn to the Lake Tahoe basin for thousands of years. The Washoe traveled up from the lowlands surrounding what is now Reno to fish, hunt, and harvest summer's woodland bounty. With the discovery of gold and silver in the mid-1800s, trails once passable only in summer became year-round routes traveled by forty-niners and the entrepreneurs—shopkeepers, tavern owners, bakers, cattlemen—who followed them. Miners' cabins, flumes, and other remnants of California's gold rush and Nevada's silver rush can be found along trails throughout the Lake Tahoe basin.

Once the booms went bust, the wildland lovers moved in—renowned wilderness advocates such as John Muir and others—and the frontier trails became paths enjoyed by tourists. Resorts sprang up around the lake, enabling visitors to explore the backcountry and then retire to sprawling estates with superlative views. Trails lead to several of these resorts, the most spectacular being Vikingsholm at the head of Emerald Bay.

These days, vacationers from San Francisco, Sacramento, and other hometowns continue to drive to Tahoe for lakeside holidays, while others call the blue heart of the Sierra home. Tourist or townie, invariably they end up outside. Invariably they want to take a hike.

The Nature of Tahoe

Tahoe's trails range from rugged and mountainous to flat and paved. Hikes in this guide cover the gamut. While by definition a Best Easy Day Hike poses little danger to the traveler,

3

knowing a few details about the nature of the Lake Tahoe region will enhance your explorations.

Lake Tahoe, at 6,224 feet, sits square in the montane zone. Lower down in this zone, the forests are dominated by Jeffrey pines and fragrant ponderosa pines, and meadows fill with blossoms in early summer. Higher up, lodgepole pine and red fir flourish. Most routes in this guide are in the montane zone, but a few brush the ecotone with the subalpine zone, where the whitebark pines and mountain hemlocks may be stunted by winter snows. The subalpine zone begins near 9,000 feet and reaches to tree line.

Take altitude into consideration when hiking at Lake Tahoe, particularly if you come from sea level. Altitude sickness is a possibility. If you or a member of your hiking party experiences any symptoms of this illness, including headache, nausea, or unusual fatigue, descend to a lower altitude immediately and seek medical attention.

The hiking season around Lake Tahoe generally stretches from the first of May to the end of October, with trails at lower elevations melting off in spring before those at higher elevations. The opening of any particular trail depends on the depth of winter's snow and the speed of snowmelt. Snowshoe hikers and cross-country skiers can travel into areas traversed by these trails during winter, weather and backcountry skills permitting.

Afternoon thunderstorms are fairly common in the summer months and taper off as the hiking season winds down. Hikers should always be prepared for changeable weather—rain, cold, snow, or heat—by wearing layers and packing waterproof gear.

Black bears are commonly seen around Lake Tahoe. If you encounter a bear on the trail, do not run. Stand still and make noise, and the bear will most likely scram. Avoid coming between a mama bear and her cubs—if you see cubs, leave the area immediately. If a bear bluff charges, stand your ground. If a bear attacks, fight back.

Support Tahoe-Truckee Trails

To learn more about trails and parklands around Lake Tahoe and neighboring communities, or to support trail building and maintenance, contact any one of the organizations listed below.

- Tahoe Rim Trail Association: (775) 298-4485; tahoerim trail.org
- Sierra State Parks Foundation: (530) 583-9911; sierra stateparks.org
- Truckee Trails Foundation: truckeetrails.org

How to Use This Guide

Each hike is described with a map and summary information that delivers the trail's vital statistics including length, difficulty, fees and permits, park hours, canine compatibility, and trail contacts.

Directions to the trailhead are provided, including the GPS coordinates of the trailhead. Starting points for driving directions are the largest communities on the lakeshore: Incline Village on the North Shore, Tahoe City on the West Shore, and South Lake Tahoe/Stateline on the South Shore. A scenic highway, variously designated CA 89, CA 28, NV 28, and US 50, circumnavigates the lake; directions to trailheads are given from this road. Directions for trails in Donner and Truckee are given from I-80.

The narrative hike description provides information about what you'll see along the trail and tidbits about natural and cultural history. A detailed route finder (Miles and Directions) sets forth mileages between significant landmarks along the trail.

How the Hikes Were Chosen

Hikes in this guide range in difficulty from flat excursions perfect for family outings to more challenging treks to highland lakes. Most trails are located in the Tahoe basin, with a few in surrounding communities like Truckee and Tahoe Donner. Wherever your starting point, I've suggested an easy day hike nearby.

While these trails are among the best, keep in mind that other trails in the same area may be better suited to your needs. Potential alternatives are suggested in the Options sections at the ends of hike descriptions.

To freshen up the fourth edition, I've added a new trail option on the North Shore and one on the South Shore. Options that appeared in earlier editions, along with summary information about how to reach them, are listed in the Options section of the nearest hike.

Selecting a Hike

"Easy" is a relative term. Some would argue no hike involving any kind of climbing is easy, but around Lake Tahoe climbs are a fact of life. Keep in mind that what you think is easy is entirely dependent on your level of fitness and the adequacy of your gear (primarily shoes). Use the trail's length as a gauge of its relative difficulty—even if climbing is involved, it won't be bad if the hike is less than 1 mile long. In addition to listing hikes that might appeal to the hiker seeking a certain experience, the Trail Finder lists the trails by level of difficulty. If you are hiking with a group, select a hike that's appropriate for the least fit/least prepared in your party.

Approximate hiking times are based on the assumption that on flat ground, most walkers average 2 miles per hour. Adjust that rate by the steepness of the terrain and your level of fitness (subtract time if you're an aerobic animal and add time if you're hiking with kids), and you have a ballpark hiking duration. Be sure to add more time if you plan to picnic or take part in other activities like birding or photography.

Trail Finder

Best Hikes for Lake Lovers
Picnic Rock
Skunk Harbor
Spooner Lake Loop
Castle Rock
Vikingsholm and Emerald Point
Pacific Crest Trail at Echo Lakes
Five Lakes Trail

Best Hikes for River/Stream Lovers
Martis Creek Wildlife Area
Sagehen Creek
Truckee River Trail

Best Hikes for Waterfalls
Galena Falls
Cascade Falls
Shirley Canyon Cascades

Best Hikes for Meadow Lovers
Tahoe Meadows Interpretive Loop
Page Meadows
Antone Meadows
Big Meadow

Best Hikes for Children
Sand Point Nature Trail
Rainbow Trail
Angora Lakes

Best Hikes for History Lovers
The Lighthouse and Rubicon Point
Vikingsholm and Emerald Point
Lake of the Sky Trail and Tallac Historic Site
Glen Alpine

Best Hikes for a Workout
Ellis Peak Trail
General Creek Loop
Five Lakes Trail

Trails by Difficulty (Easiest to Hardest)
Sand Point Nature Trail
Rainbow Trail
Angora Lakes
Tahoe Meadows Interpretive Loop
Spooner Lake Loop
Lam Watah Historic Trail
Sagehen Creek
Lakeside Interpretive Trail at Donner Lake
Lake of the Sky Trail and Tallac Historic Site
Shirley Canyon Cascades
Skunk Harbor
Eagle Lake
Truckee River Trail
Castle Rock
Picnic Rock
Page Meadows
Big Meadow
Pacific Crest Trail at Echo Lakes
Martis Creek Wildlife Area
Glen Alpine
General Creek Loop

Antone Meadows
Galena Falls
Cascade Falls
Vikingsholm and Emerald Point
The Lighthouse and Rubicon Point
Cathedral Lake
Five Lakes Trail
Ellis Peak Trail

Map Legend

⑧	Interstate Highway
⑲	US Highway
㉞	State Highway
	Local Road
= = = = = =	Unpaved Road
	Featured Trail
- - - - - - -	Trail
‖‖‖‖‖‖‖‖	Boardwalk
- · - · - · -	State Line
~	River/Creek
⬭	Body of Water
	Marsh/Swamp
	State Park/Wilderness Area
🪑	Bench
⛵	Boat Launch
⌣	Bridge
Δ	Camping
•—•	Gate
❷	Information Center
🗼	Lighthouse
Ⓟ	Parking
▲	Peak
🅿	Picnic Area
■	Point of Interest/Structure
🚻	Restroom
○	Town
⓫	Trailhead
🔍	Viewpoint/Overlook
≋	Waterfall

1 Lakeside Interpretive Trail at Donner Lake

Lake Tahoe gets all the glory, but this satellite lake, also deep and blue, is highlighted by an interpretive trail that shines a spotlight on both the spectacular setting and the remarkable, disturbing history of Donner Pass.

Start: Parking lot for the picnic area near the gauging station. You can also start at the park visitor center.

Distance: 2.4 miles out and back

Hiking time: About 2 hours

Difficulty: Easy

Trail surface: Dirt singletrack, barrier-free

Best seasons: Spring, summer, fall

Other trail users: None

Trail amenities: Restrooms, picnic facilities, camping

Canine compatibility: Leashed dogs permitted in developed picnic areas, but not at China Cove

Fees and permits: Day-use fee to enter the park.

Schedule: Visitor center (museum) hours are from 10 a.m. to 5 p.m. daily.

Maps: USGS Truckee and Norden CA; park trail map available at the entrance station and on an information board at the entrance

Trail contact: Donner Memorial State Park, 12593 Donner Pass Rd., Truckee, CA 96161; (530) 582-7892; www.parks.ca.gov. Sierra State Parks Foundation (info about Tahoe-Truckee area state parks), sierrastateparks.org.

Other: While at the park you can visit the Emigrant Trail Museum (open 10 a.m. to 5 p.m. daily); the Pioneer Monument; and the Murphy family cabin site (a remnant of the Donner expedition). Contact ReserveCalifornia (800-444-7275; reservecalifornia .com) for camping reservations.

Finding the trailhead: Take CA 89 from Tahoe City or CA 28 from Kings Beach to I-80 in Truckee. Head west on I-80 to the Donner Pass Road exit (about 0.7 mile west of the CA 89 interchange with I-80). Go left (south) on Donner Pass Road to the well-signed park entrance on the left (south). The trailhead is in the parking lot for the picnic area. Follow the park road past the entrance station and across the bridge, staying right at the gated campground road. The signed lot is on the right. GPS: N39 19.415' / W120 14.220'

The Hike

The story of the Donner Party is one of the grimmest in the history of the American West. Trapped by deep snow below the summit of what would become known as Donner Pass in the winter of 1846–1847, embattled emigrants who'd already encountered a number of hardships on their cross-country passage endured madness, despair, and cannibalism in their fight to survive. More than thirty souls perished in the scattered cabins and camps established around Donner Lake; two of those cabin sites are preserved within the park boundaries.

No worries of such trauma on this hike, however—it's barely long or arduous enough to warrant a pause for a handful of trail mix. The route also sheds light on how this rugged high country was eventually rendered habitable, with interpretive panels describing settlement and industry in the area and the construction of the railroad and highway that would eventually make travel over the infamous pass relatively easy, even in winter.

The trailhead is at the picnic area at the Donner Creek dam; you can also start at the park's visitor center. Begin at a small sign near the gauging station on Donner Creek, with the blue-green lake welling up alongside the dirt track. It roughly parallels the park road, with access to lakeside beaches, picnic grounds, and restrooms along most of its length. Expect some road noise from the nearby interstate and park road—and the occasional rumble and whistle blow of a train riding high on the mountainside to the south—but you'll also be able to hear birds chirping in the lakeside brambles and the wind whirring through the treetops.

Tile mosaics touting the benefits of recycling, healthy forests, and responsible development, created by local fifth-graders, line the trailside at the 0.3-mile mark. The open forest allows glimpses of the gray granite heights of Donner Peak and Schallenberger Ridge to the south and west. A chain of picnic areas includes a prime spot on a sand spit on the southeast shore, with views of lakeshore cabins on the north side.

The interpretive signs at the west end of the trail focus on the human and natural history of the area, touching on the role fire plays in the maintenance of forest health, the geologic origins of the Sierra Nevada, the Native Americans that summered in the area, early European settlement, construction of a wagon road over the pass in the 1850s, and completion of the interstate in the 1960s.

China Cove's crescent beach, with great views across the lake to the western peaks and ridges, is at trail's end. Picnic tables and restrooms make this the perfect place for lunch and relaxing. Return as you came or follow the park road back to the trailhead.

Lakeside Interpretive Trail at Donner Lake

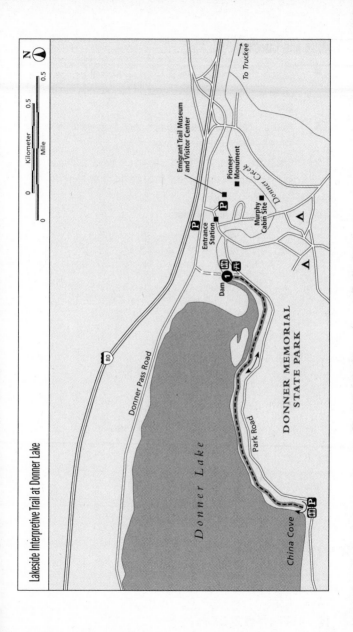

Miles and Directions

0.0   Start in the picnic area parking lot at the trail sign near the gauging station. Head southwest on the obvious waterside path.

0.5   Pass a picnic site on a sand spit, then more picnic sites on the left (south) side of the trail.

1.2   Reach the beach at China Cove. Take a break and read the last of the interpretive signs, then retrace your steps to the trailhead.

2.4   Arrive back at the trailhead.

2 Sagehen Creek

A lovely trail leads through wildflower-filled meadows and woodlands to the shoreline of an arm of Stampede Reservoir.

Start: Trailhead alongside CA 89 north of Truckee
Distance: 4.8 miles out and back
Hiking time: 2-3 hours
Difficulty: Easy
Trail surface: Dirt singletrack
Best seasons: Late spring, summer, fall
Other trail users: Mountain bikers, trail runners
Trail amenities: Parking for about 15 cars in a roadside pullout
Canine compatibility: Leashed dogs permitted

Fees and permits: None
Schedule: Sunrise to sunset daily
Maps: USGS Hobart Mills CA
Trail contact: Tahoe National Forest, Truckee Ranger District, 10811 Stockrest Springs Rd., Truckee, CA 96161; (530) 587-3558; www.fs.usda.gov/tahoe
Special considerations: The meadowlands and creek foster a healthy population of insects in spring. To enjoy the wildflower display without losing pints of blood, use bug juice and dress appropriately.

Finding the trailhead: From the junction of CA 267/CA 89 and I-80 in Truckee, head north on CA 89 toward Sierraville and Graeagle. The unsigned parking area for the trailhead is 7.3 miles north of the junction with the interstate, at the bottom of a substantial hill and on the right side of the roadway. GPS: N39 26.040' / W120 12.297'

The Hike

This gentle ramble leads through meadowlands alongside Sagehen Creek to a remote arm of the Stampede Reservoir. The trail is flat and straightforward, with plenty of wildflowers in season and wonderful views across the reservoir year-round.

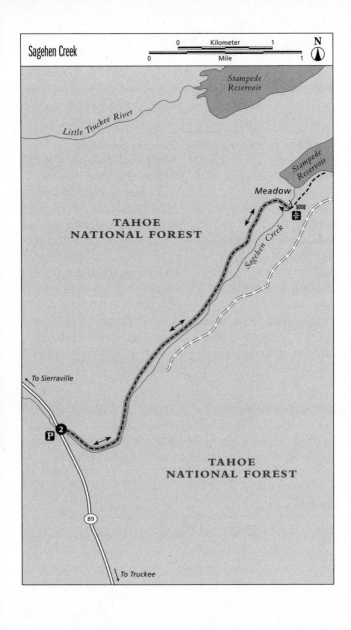

Sagehen Creek

0   Kilometer   1

0   Mile   1

N

Little Truckee River

Stampede Reservoir

Stampede Reservoir

Meadow

TAHOE NATIONAL FOREST

Sagehen Creek

To Sierraville

P 2

TAHOE NATIONAL FOREST

89

To Truckee

Begin by rambling along the creek, avoiding the side paths leading down to the stream. Willows and small aspen crowd the path. Bend to the northeast and the creek drainage widens, with skunk cabbage growing amid grasses in the gentle valley.

At about the 1-mile mark, as the trail traverses above Sagehen Creek, you can look down right onto a shallow pond, which may be dry in late season or under drought conditions. Young pines have begun to colonize the grasslands, though the evergreens grow relatively thick on the steeper slope to the left.

The path widens to doubletrack as it heads across a broadening meadow, with views of Stampede Reservoir ahead. Pass into parklike stands of evergreens. Timbers form a bridge over a side stream. Continue through the grasses to a plank bridge that spans the main channel of Sagehen Creek.

The turnaround point is a bench offering great views of the quiet waters of Stampede Reservoir. An overgrown trail continues through the marshy grasslands, which you can explore if you desire. Otherwise, return as you came.

Miles and Directions

0.0   Start by heading down the trail alongside Sagehen Creek.

1.0   Pass a small, shallow pond.

1.7   The trail separates into a doubletrack and enters a broad meadow.

2.3   Cross a bridge made of hewn timber.

2.4   Cross the main channel of Sagehen Creek. Enjoy views of Stampede Reservoir from a bench, then return as you came.

4.8   Arrive back at the trailhead.

Options: The Northwoods Interpretive Nature Trail, a second-edition favorite that also lies just outside Truckee, explores the meadows and woodlands surrounding Trout Creek within the Tahoe Donner subdivision. Interpretive signs along the track describe bears and birds of prey, wildflowers and willows, trout and trees. The boardwalk section is particularly inviting, with wildflowers flourishing in late spring and summer. The 2.1-mile loop, which takes about an hour to complete, is composed of singletrack and boardwalks and is easy to follow. The trail is suitable for children and can be traversed from late spring through fall (watch for bugs in early season). Leashed dogs are permitted.

To reach the trailhead from downtown Truckee, head west on I-80 to the Donner Pass Road exit (about 0.7 mile west of the CA 89 interchange). Go right (east) on Donner Pass Road for 0.4 mile to Northwoods Boulevard. Turn left (north) onto Northwoods Boulevard and go 1.4 miles to the Northwoods Clubhouse and parking lot on the right (east). The signed trailhead is in the northwest corner of the clubhouse parking lot. GPS: N39 20.624' / W120 12.991'

Beyond the Northwoods Trail, an expanding network of multiuse trails offers a variety of opportunities for exploration throughout Tahoe Donner. Many follow fire roads and offer great views of Donner Lake and the Truckee River valley. For details about access, download a trail map at www.tahoedonner.com/amenities/amenities/trails/. For more information, contact the Tahoe Donner Association Member Services Office; (530) 587-9400; tahoedonner.com.

For more information on Truckee area trails, visit the Truckee Trails Foundation at truckeetrails.org. The Truckee Chamber of Commerce also maintains an online database of information about the mountain town, including where to eat, where to stay, and local events. Visit the site at truckee .com, or contact the chamber by calling (530) 587-8808.

3 Martis Creek Wildlife Area

Wildlife abounds around Martis Creek, thriving in the biggest expanse of meadow and marshland in the Tahoe area. The birds dominate, chirping, flitting, and soaring over the landscape. Whether you love birds or not, exploring the grassland is a heavenly hiking experience.

Start: Martis Creek Wildlife Area parking lot off CA 267

Distance: 4.2-mile loop

Hiking time: About 2.5 hours

Difficulty: Moderate due only to length

Trail surface: Dirt singletrack, boardwalk

Best seasons: Late spring, summer, fall

Other trail users: Trail runners, mountain bikers on the Tomkins Memorial Trail (not permitted on the Martis Creek Trail)

Trail amenities: Information kiosk with maps, picnic facilities

Canine compatibility: Leashed dogs permitted on the Tomkins Memorial Trail. Please pick up after your pet; bags are provided at the trailhead. Do not leave bags along the trail.

Fees and permits: None

Schedule: Sunrise to sunset daily

Maps: USGS Martis Peak and Truckee CA; maps are also posted at the trailhead and along the route.

Trail contact: US Army Corps of Engineers; (530) 587-8113; www.spk.usace.army.mil/Locations/Sacramento-District-Parks/Martis-Creek-Lake/

Special considerations: Avoid the fragile Martis Creek Trail if possible, which has been impacted by overuse. This route passes through an important Washoe Indian heritage area. Removal of artifacts and/or damaging historic or prehistoric sites is prohibited by law. The Army Corps of Engineers, which oversees the trail, also maintains a campground across CA 267, north of the wildlife area.

Finding the trailhead: From the signalized junction of CA 28 and CA 267 in Kings Beach, follow CA 267 for 8.3 miles, over Brockway Summit, to the signed Martis Creek Wildlife Area turnoff on the left (south). Follow the gravel access road for 0.1 mile to the trailhead. From I-80 in Truckee, take exit 188B/CA 267 toward Kings Beach and head south for 3 miles, past the main entrance for Martis Creek Lake, to the trailhead access road on the right. Parking is limited; if spaces are full, park along the access road or visit another day. GPS: N39 18.096' / W120 07.840'

The Hike

Willow-lined Martis Creek cuts a sinuous path through acres of wetland meadow southeast of Truckee, carving deep into the turf, its branches watering a springtime bloom of wildflowers and providing sustenance for a variety of creatures.

The birds are most prominent, their songs loud enough to be heard over the hum of cars passing on the nearby highway. Songbirds flit from willow to wild rose to thatch of grass in flashes of brown, black, red, yellow, and sometimes vivid blue. Watch for raptors stilling in the clear mountain air and swallows shooting in and out of the highway underpass. Fish, amphibians, and mammals large and small also call the Martis Creek Wildlife Area home.

The Tomkins Memorial Trail arcs through the sanctuary in a long loop that first immerses hikers in the meadow ecosystem, then in the forest that cloaks the slopes of the Northstar ski resort's Lookout Mountain. The hospitable meadowland has known human habitation for 10,000 years or more, but where once you may have walked among hunters and gatherers, these days you will never be far from modern civilization, whether private homes, puttering golfers, or the occasional airplane approaching or leaving the regional airport.

Martis Creek Wildlife Area

MARTIS CREEK LAKE NATIONAL RECREATION AREA

MARTIS CREEK WILDLIFE AREA

To Kings Beach

Gumba's Crossing

Golf Course

Tomkins Memorial Trail

Martis Creek

Martis Creek Trail

Pappe's Bridge

N

0   0.5   Kilometer
0   0.5   Mile

The Tomkins Memorial Trail loop is described clockwise. The trail parallels the highway at the outset, following a broad track easily shared with other trail users. At one of many named bridges spanning the wandering creek and its tributaries, the trail breaks south toward Northstar, traversing sometimes soggy meadow via boardwalks and singletrack.

The metal roofs of private homes glint through the trees as you approach the base of the mountain. The trail curves west along the edge of the golf course, then through the forest at the bottom of the ski area. A brief foray into the woodland ends back in the meadow, where the Tomkins Memorial Trail hitches up with the Martis Creek Trail.

The track along Martis Creek has been, according to its advocates, loved to death. The onetime cattle path is the subject of ongoing rehabilitation efforts, with access to its eroding, willow-choked banks discouraged. It's best to finish the meadow tour on the Tomkins Trail, using a boardwalk and well-maintained track. A bench along this final stretch offers hikers a chance to rest and look down across the creek and valley. The Tomkins Trail meets the Martis Creek Trail below the parking area; a short, easy climb leads out of the bottomlands and back to the trailhead.

Miles and Directions

0.0   Start on the signed Tomkins Memorial Trail, following the broad path that parallels the highway.

0.5   Cross Frank's Fish Bridge, the first of many named spans.

0.8   Reach Gumba's Crossing. Cross the bridge, then head southeast across the boardwalk.

1.0   Cross the Green Team's Bridge, then the Broken Bridge.

1.4 Pass under power lines and curl along the fenced boundary between the wildlife area and the golf course.

1.6 At a break in the fence, marked by a trail sign, go right (northwest) to continue the loop. The left-hand path leads up into the neighborhood.

1.9 Pass a picnic table shaded by massive twin Jeffrey pines, then cross Michael Cousin's Bridge.

2.2 Now in woodland, pass several junctions with social trails leading back into the neighborhood. Stay right at the junctions on the obvious Tomkins Memorial Trail.

2.6 A picnic table and trail map at the edge of a small meadow mark a sharp turn in the trail.

2.9 Reach a bench at the interface between meadow and woodland.

3.1 Pass through scrubland to another trail sign. Ignore side trails, staying straight (west) on the broad main track.

3.3 Arrive at Pappe's Bridge, where there is a picnic table and a trail sign. Take the Tomkins Memorial Trail, which continues straight via a boardwalk. The signed Martis Creek Trail breaks to the right (northeast).

4.1 Meet the Martis Creek Trail below the trailhead and climb toward the parking area.

4.2 Arrive back at the trailhead.

4 Picnic Rock

From a perch atop this rock outcrop accessed via the Tahoe Rim Trail off Brockway Summit, hikers are rewarded with panoramic vistas of the lake, the Tahoe basin, and the Sierra crest.

Start: Roadside trailhead below Brockway Summit
Distance: 3.2 miles out and back
Hiking time: 1–2 hours
Difficulty: Moderate
Trail surface: Dirt
Best seasons: Late spring, summer, fall
Other trail users: The occasional mountain biker
Trail amenities: None
Canine compatibility: Leashed dogs permitted
Fees and permits: None

Schedule: Sunrise to sunset daily
Maps: USGS Mount Rose NV; Tom Harrison Recreation Map of Lake Tahoe; National Geographic 803 Lake Tahoe Basin Trail Map
Trail contact: US Forest Service Lake Tahoe Basin Management Unit, Forest Supervisor's Office, 35 College Dr., South Lake Tahoe, CA 96150; (530) 543-2600; www.fs.usda.gov/ltbmu. Tahoe Rim Trail Association, 128 Market St., Ste. 3E/PO Box 3267, Stateline, NV 89449; (775) 298-4485; tahoerimtrail.org.

Finding the trailhead: From Kings Beach, drive 2.7 miles northwest on CA 267 to the obvious Tahoe Rim Trail parking area alongside the road. The trailhead is on the north side of the highway, across from the parking area. GPS: N39 15.515' / W120 03.875'

The Hike

A steady but easy climb up the Tahoe Rim Trail (TRT) near Brockway Summit leads to amazing panoramic views of Lake Tahoe and the Sierra crest. On a clear day the jagged

Picnic Rock

0   Kilometer   0.25
0   Mile   0.25

N

Tahoe Rim Trail

Picnic
Rock ▲

Tahoe Rim Trail

To Truckee

267

4
P

To Kings
Beach

267

line of the basin's rim separates the blue of the lake from the blue of the sky, setting up postcard- and guidebook-perfect photographic possibilities. Pick a spot on a rock outcrop, have a seat, and savor.

The trail begins just off CA 267. Climb a short section of four-wheel-drive roadway to the trailhead proper and stay left on the signed TRT. Sweeping switchbacks with long traverses climb gently away from the highway. The open woodlands permit tree-filtered lake views at the outset. Road noise is constant, but wind in the treetops provides a buffer, and the sounds of motors fade as the route bends northward and the woods grow denser.

After a little more than a mile, the spur to the Picnic Rock viewpoint breaks to the left. Another pair of switchbacks eases the final pitch to the rock outcrops, which sprawl across a rolling ridgeline. The trail splinters among the rocks, which are user-friendly and perfect for picture-taking, resting in the sunshine, and . . . well, picnicking. Don't forget to turn around: Gazing north and west, the granite slopes and valleys of the Sierra present a lovely panorama as well.

After you've taken it all in, retrace your steps to the trailhead.

Miles and Directions

0.0   Start on the four-wheel-drive road on the north side of CA 267.

0.1   At the Tahoe Rim Trail signboard, go left onto the trail.

1.3   Go left onto the signed spur trail.

1.6   Reach Picnic Rock. Take in the views, then return as you came.

3.2   Arrive back at the trailhead.

Options: Continue northbound on the Tahoe Rim Trail to access the Martis Peak Lookout, Relay Peak, and the Tahoe Meadows TRT trailhead. Heading south on the TRT from the Brockway Summit trailhead leads to Watson Lake, a camp spot for thru-hikers and others, and then to the Tahoe City trailhead.

5 Tahoe Meadows Interpretive Loop

Meandering through a lovely meadow beneath the summits of Slide Mountain and Mount Rose, this flat, friendly interpretive route is perfect for families, wildflower enthusiasts, and view seekers.

Start: Tahoe Rim trailhead parking lot, just off NV 431 below the Mount Rose crest
Distance: 1.3-mile loop
Hiking time: About 1 hour
Difficulty: Easy
Trail surface: Wide dirt pathway, bridges
Best seasons: Summer, fall
Other trail users: None
Trail amenities: Information signs, restrooms (open in summer)
Canine compatibility: Leashed dogs permitted
Fees and permits: None
Schedule: Sunrise to sunset daily

Maps: USGS Mount Rose NV; Tom Harrison Recreation Map of Lake Tahoe; National Geographic 803 Lake Tahoe Basin Trail Map
Trail contact: US Forest Service Lake Tahoe Basin Management Unit, Forest Supervisor's Office, 35 College Dr., South Lake Tahoe, CA 96150; (530) 543-2600; www.fs.usda.gov/ltbmu. Tahoe Rim Trail Association, 128 Market St., Ste. 3E/PO Box 3267, Stateline, NV 89449; (775) 298-4485; tahoerimtrail.org.
Other: The route lies within the Humboldt-Toiyabe National Forest.

Finding the trailhead: From the intersection of NV 28 and Village Boulevard in Incline Village, head west on NV 28 to NV 431 (the scenic Mount Rose Highway). At the roundabout, go right (northeast) onto NV 431 for 7.3 miles to the signed trailhead on the right (east). From Tahoe City, follow CA 28 (which becomes NV 28 once you cross the state line in Crystal Bay) for 14 miles to the roundabout junction with NV 431. Go north on NV 431 to the trailhead parking area. If no parking is available in the lot, park in the pullout on NV 431. GPS: N39 18.433' / W119 54.436'

The Hike

Easy and scenic, the Tahoe Meadows Interpretive Loop circles through a verdant grassland rich with wildflowers at nearly 8,700 feet, offering access to stands of stately evergreens, a chance to study a habitat that lies dormant under a thick blanket of snow for much of the year, and vistas of high ridges that stretch south to Lake Tahoe and up to the stony summits of Slide Mountain and Mount Rose. Though the Mount Rose Highway, a lovely and popular drive, is never distant, scenery and altitude qualify this as a premier alpine short hike.

A trail sign behind the restroom marks the start. Though this section of the Tahoe Rim Trail climbs gently at the outset, it's never strenuous, making it the perfect destination for families discovering the wonders of wildland treadways. The first part of the trail is also accessible to hardy wheelchair users.

Follow the well-groomed dirt path into the meadow; at an interpretive sign and boardwalk/bridge, the trail splits, forming the loop. Stay left (north), as the signs indicate, traveling in a clockwise direction. The path merges into a patch of pavement, then reverts to natural surface as it traces the edge of the meadow. Altitude-stunted evergreens briefly block the meadow views, then the route traces the interface of forest and grassland as it approaches the head of the meadow.

At a trail sign, diverge from the Tahoe Rim Trail, which continues northeast toward Mount Rose. Stay right (east) on

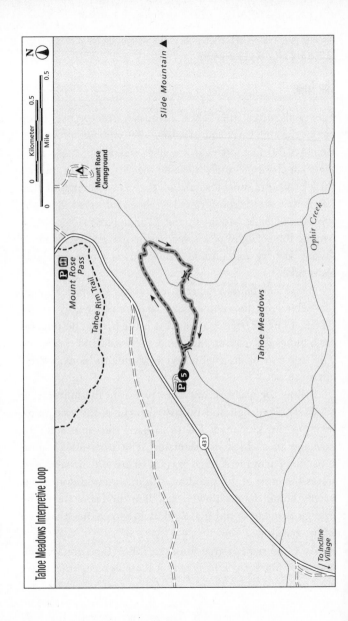

Tahoe Meadows Interpretive Loop

Mount Rose Pass

Tahoe Rim Trail

Mount Rose Campground

431

To Incline Village

Tahoe Meadows

Ophir Creek

Slide Mountain

N

Kilometer   0.5

Mile   0.5

the loop trail, curving south toward Lake Tahoe and entering a mature woodland. Interpretive signs along this stretch describe frogs and fish, butterflies and birds, human habitation and hibernation. Bridges span the stream that waters the meadow, and you can spot the tiny fish that somehow survive at these heights.

The trail emerges from the forest to cross small bridges and boardwalks in the moist meadow. Views down the mountain open into a blue void: the Tahoe basin, with the lake 2,000 feet below and out of sight. Close the loop at the bridge and trail sign, then retrace your steps back to the trailhead.

Miles and Directions

0.0   Start at the information sign.

0.1   The trail splits at an interpretive sign and bridge. Take the left leg, traveling in a clockwise direction.

0.5   Diverge from the Tahoe Rim Trail, which continues northeast toward Mount Rose. Go right (east) on the interpretive trail.

0.8   Pass a trail marker and cross a bridge.

1.2   Reach the trail junction to close the loop.

1.3   Arrive back at the trailhead.

6 Galena Falls

A lovely stretch of the Tahoe Rim Trail traverses the base of Tamarack Peak to Galena Falls, at the head of a willowy valley sheltered by the pink slopes of Mount Rose.

Start: Tahoe Rim Trail/Mount Rose trailhead at the summit of the Mount Rose Highway (NV 431)

Distance: 4.8 miles out and back

Hiking time: 3–4 hours

Difficulty: Moderate due to elevation and distance

Trail surface: Dirt singletrack

Best seasons: Summer, fall

Other trail users: None

Trail amenities: Parking, restrooms, picnic facilities, trash cans, information signboards

Canine compatibility: Dogs must be on leash within 1 mile of the trailhead. Dogs are permitted in the Mount Rose Wilderness; owners must keep them under control and clean up their waste.

Fees and permits: None

Schedule: Sunrise to sunset daily

Maps: USGS Mount Rose CA; National Geographic 803 Lake Tahoe Basin Trail Map

Trail contact: US Forest Service Lake Tahoe Basin Management Unit, Forest Supervisor's Office, 35 College Dr., South Lake Tahoe, CA 96150; (530) 543-2600; www.fs.usda.gov/ltbmu. Tahoe Rim Trail Association, 128 Market St., Ste. 3E/PO Box 3267, Stateline, NV 89449; (775) 298-4485; tahoerimtrail.org.

Finding the trailhead: From the junction of NV 28 and NV 431 (the Mount Rose Highway) in Incline Village (at the roundabout), go north on NV 431. Travel the scenic highway for 8 miles to the summit parking area. The trailhead is located behind the restrooms and information signboards. GPS: N39 18.790' / W119 53.859'

The Hike

Mount Rose is an obvious hiker's target. It is among the highest ramparts of the Carson Range and, with its neighbor Slide Mountain, is an iconic element of the Lake Tahoe basin's north rim. Tucked away near the base of the mountain climb proper is another, easier goal: Galena Falls, a whitewater cascade about 50 feet high.

Located at about 9,000 feet, the falls are at the head of the Galena Creek drainage. Flowing eastward, the creek waters a widening meadow of willow and wildflowers before beginning a long tumble into Reno, more than 4,000 feet below. Mount Rose, a long-extinct volcano with distinctive pink-hued slopes, towers to the northeast.

The hike begins with an easy, relatively flat traverse on the Tahoe Rim Trail (TRT), with views opening across marshy Tahoe Meadows toward the lake basin. Highway noise drifts up to the route, but once you top a knoll and begin to hike along northeast-facing slopes below Tamarack Peak, plunging into woodland, you won't be able to discern the hum of engines from the wind ruffling the treetops.

The north- and east-facing slopes of Tamarack may hold snow late in the season, which is the only challenge hikers may face on the long, rolling traverse through thick evergreens. Clearings allow great views down steep ravines into the Truckee Meadows. A short, lumpy cliff face is visible to the right (east) at about the halfway point; the route gently descends from here toward the falls.

The trail has a wilder feel by the time you reach the junction of the TRT to Relay Peak and the trail to the summit of Mount Rose. Galena Falls, vigorous in early season and mellowing as the summer draws on, tumbles down a broken

Galena Falls

0 ——— Kilometer ——— 1

0 ——— Mile ——— 1

N

Mount Rose
10,709 ft.

Mount Rose Trail

Galena Creek

Galena Falls

Tahoe Rim Trail
to Relay Peak

Tahoe Rim Trail/Mount Rose Trail

Tamarack Peak

Tamarack Lake

431

To Reno

P

6

Mount Rose Hwy

P

Tahoe Meadows
Interpretive Loop

To Incline Village

rock face, the stone brown and blocky behind the cascade. Visit in late spring and early summer for the best wildflower display in the meadow. Find a seat on a dry rock and enjoy the falls and flowers before returning as you came.

Miles and Directions

0.0   Start at the Mount Rose trailhead at the summit parking area on NV 431, following the Tahoe Rim Trail and the signed trail to Mount Rose.

0.1   At the trail Y (the junction of the Tahoe Rim Trail heading south into Tahoe Meadows), go right (up the stairs) on the TRT/Mount Rose Trail.

0.5   Top a knoll and check out the views south across Lake Tahoe and northeast into the Truckee Meadows and Washoe Valley.

1.4   Round a knob with views of a lumpy, wooded ridge.

2.4   Reach Galena Falls and the junction of the TRT to Relay Peak and the trail to Mount Rose. This is the turnaround point, though if you desire you can continue on to the summit of Mount Rose, or follow the TRT along the lake basin rim. Otherwise, return as you came.

4.8   Arrive back at the trailhead.

Options: For those who crave summits, the top of Mount Rose appears tantalizingly close. Another 2.4 miles of incessant climbing along the well-marked Mount Rose Trail leads to the apex, where you can enjoy panoramic views into Nevada and down onto Lake Tahoe. Be prepared for a long, hard hike, however; there's not only mileage to consider but also altitude. The summit is at 10,776 feet, and the climbing doesn't let up beyond Galena Falls.

If you are staying in Incline Village, the best close-in option for a quick leg stretch or workout is the Incline Fitness Trail, which follows a winding route through a patch of forest just off Ski Beach. This 1.1-mile loop is lined with exercise stations and navigates a strip of forest between a pair of streams. While not a wilderness hike, given that the Village Green, the Hyatt Regency hotel, and private homes are visible from the trail, the pocket of woodland provides a nice quick escape. Start at the signed trailhead at the Aspen Grove Community Center on Lakeshore Boulevard (GPS: N39 14.410' / W119 56.746'). A network of walking trails also follows Lakeshore Boulevard and winds through the neighborhoods of the village. Mostly paved, these paths connect businesses, schools, and recreation sites.

Midway between the mountaintop and the beach lies another North Shore option. The Incline/Tyrolean Downhill is popular with both hikers and mountain bikers, and it offers great lake views, a stretch along a vibrant mountain stream, and a thigh-pumping climb. Because there's no easy parking at the base of the trail in Incline, most hikers do this route either upside-down, or one way, starting at the trailhead on the Mount Rose Highway and ending in Incline, where they've left a shuttle car. The route is 5.5 miles out and back (2.75 miles as a shuttle), follows a dirt trail, and dogs are permitted. The upper trailhead is in a parking pullout 3.9 miles up NV 431 from the roundabout (GPS: N39 16.115' / W119 55.835').

7 Sand Point Nature Trail

Take a quick stroll along the boardwalk at Sand Harbor and indulge in unimpeded views across Lake Tahoe. The path also hooks around rocky shoreline coves, and interpretive signs describe some of the components that make the lake's environment beautiful and unique. The loop is perfect for families.

Start: Informational kiosk near the restrooms at Sand Point
Distance: 0.4-mile loop
Hiking time: About 30 minutes
Difficulty: Easy
Trail surface: Boardwalk, brick walkway
Best seasons: Spring, summer, fall
Other trail users: None
Trail amenities: Restrooms, water, visitor center, gift shop, trash cans
Canine compatibility: Dogs not permitted
Fees and permits: Day-use fee
Schedule: The park is open from 8 a.m. to 9 p.m. daily from Memorial Day to Labor Day. From May 1 to Memorial Day and from Labor Day to Sept 30, hours are from 8 a.m. to 7 p.m. daily. From Oct 1 to Apr 30, hours are from 8 a.m. to 5 p.m. daily.
Maps: USGS Marlette Lake NV, but no map is needed.
Trail contact: Lake Tahoe–Nevada State Park, PO Box 6116, Incline Village, NV 89452; (775) 831-0494; parks.nv.gov/parks/sand-harbor/
Other: Sand Harbor accommodates swimming, boating, and picnic facilities. The park also hosts the annual Lake Tahoe Shakespeare Festival in late summer; the amphitheater is cupped inside the trail loop. Sand Harbor is also a popular spot for scuba diving in the lake, with wetsuit-clad divers exploring the underwater rock formations.
Special considerations: The trail is wheelchair accessible. The parking lots fill by midmorning on summer days, restricting access to the park and trail. The Tahoe Transportation District runs a shuttle between Sand Harbor and Incline Village daily during the high season; visit tahoetransportation.org for details.

Finding the trailhead: From the junction of NV 28 and Village Boulevard in Incline Village, follow NV 28 south along Lake Tahoe's East Shore for 4.8 miles to the signed park entrance on the right (west). GPS: N39 11.849' / W119 55.886'

The Hike

Visit Sand Harbor early on a weekday and you might find the typically crowded beach nearly deserted, though the parking lot may bustle with divers preparing to explore the nearby shoreline. You'll also likely have the boardwalk that circles Sand Point all to yourself, a rare treat sweetened with amazing vistas. On a typical summer morning, the smooth lake surface reflects a sky of uninterrupted blue, and the morning sun casts defining shadows on rock formations cluttering the lakeshore.

But while an early walk holds special appeal, the Sand Point Nature Trail is delightful any time of day. Super-easy, wheelchair and stroller accessible, and lined with interpretive signs, the route is a fine addition to any East Shore visit.

Begin on the north side of the restrooms at an informational kiosk, stepping onto an elevated walkway constructed of recycled plastic boards. The boardwalk overlooks a small rocky cove where divers enter the cold water and kayakers launch. Ponderosa pines, snow fences, interpretive signs, and jumbles of granite line the route.

As you round Sand Point (traveling counterclockwise), the trail surface changes to brick, and short side trails lead to vista points overlooking tiny coves guarded by granite boulders. The last section of the trail looks down on the huge sandy beach, often thickly blanketed with sunbathers and colorful shade umbrellas. The trail ends in front of the

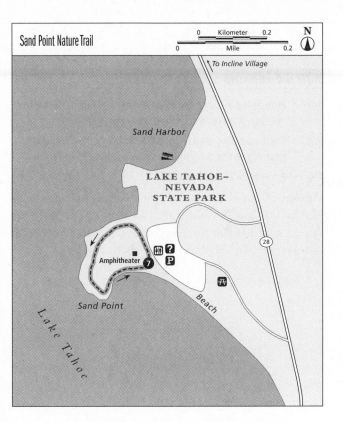

Sand Point Nature Trail

Sand Harbor

To Incline Village

LAKE TAHOE–
NEVADA
STATE PARK

Amphitheater **7**

Sand Point

Beach

Lake Tahoe

28

N

Kilometer 0.2

Mile 0.2

restrooms near the entrance to the amphitheater, home of the annual Shakespeare festival.

Miles and Directions

0.0   Start at the kiosk on the north side of the restrooms, traveling the loop in a counterclockwise direction.

0.2   Short side trails lead to vista points. Explore the shoreline, returning to the main trail and continuing the circuit.

0.4   Arrive back at the trailhead.

Option: A paved bike path linking Incline Village to Sand Harbor was under construction in late season 2018, and slated for completion by the end of the year. The lakeside pathway will hug the shoreline for about 3 miles.

8 Skunk Harbor

An unfortunate name for a favorite trail, Skunk Harbor is no stinker. Instead, a broad, steep track leads to a secluded bay where Tahoe's clear water washes onto a crescent beach, melting from indigo to turquoise to gold as it approaches shore.

Start: Unmarked turnout on the lake side of NV 28. Look for a green gate.
Distance: 3.0 miles out and back
Hiking time: About 2 hours
Difficulty: Moderate due to elevation change of more than 600 feet
Trail surface: Dirt access road
Best seasons: Late spring, summer, fall
Other trail users: The occasional mountain biker
Trail amenities: None. Limited parking (for about 5 cars) is at the gate/trailhead, with parking for 10–12 more cars in a paved pullout about 100 yards north (uphill) of the gate.
Canine compatibility: Leashed dogs permitted

Fees and permits: None
Schedule: Sunrise to sunset daily
Maps: USGS Marlette Lake NV; Lake Tahoe Basin Management Unit Map; National Geographic 803 Lake Tahoe Basin Trail Map; Tom Harrison Recreation Map of Lake Tahoe
Trail contact: US Forest Service Lake Tahoe Basin Management Unit, Forest Supervisor's Office, 35 College Dr., South Lake Tahoe, CA 96150; (530) 543-2600; www.fs.usda.gov/ltbmu
Other: Limited parking and the lack of signage make the trailhead a challenge to find but help ensure the route will not be crowded.

Finding the trailhead: From the junction of NV 28 and Village Boulevard in Incline Village, follow NV 28 south along the East Shore for 9.3 miles to the unsigned trailhead on the right (west/lakeside). From the intersection of US 50 and CA 89 in South Lake Tahoe, drive 17.9 miles north on US 50 to its intersection with NV 28 near Spooner Summit. Turn left (north) onto NV 28 and go about 2.4 miles to the trailhead, which is on the left side of the highway. A green gate tucked below the highway blocks vehicle access to the trail. GPS: N39 07.717' / W119 55.878'

The Hike

As if a sandy beach, sunbaked rocks, and cool, clear water weren't enough to draw hikers down to Skunk Harbor, the little cove is also the site of the picturesque Newhall House, built in 1923 as a wedding gift from George Newhall to his wife, Caroline. A plaque explains the origin and preservation of the house, but the true monument is the rustic structure itself, all stonework and peaked roofs and heavy wooden window frames. Peek through barred windows into the bare interior, then spread a picnic on one of the verandas, enjoying wonderful views that open through the harbor onto the lake.

Swimming and picnicking are popular activities for those who venture down the steep access road to the harbor. Powerboats sometimes drop anchor in the cove, sharing the amenities with those who've arrived on foot. But even with some coming by land and others by water, the destination is seldom crowded. An "upside-down" hike, with the climb on the return trip, Skunk Harbor allows you to prepare for the ascent by enjoying a long lakeside rest.

To begin, pass the gate and head down on the paved, then dirt, roadway. The old road flattens and circles through a drainage, then traverses the mountainside. From the traverse you can catch views of Slaughterhouse Canyon and the lake beyond.

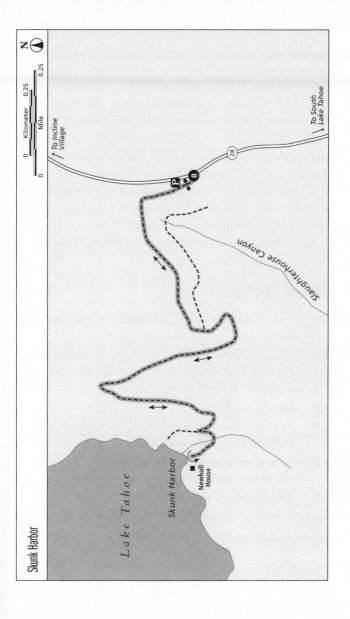

Skunk Harbor

N

Lake Tahoe

Skunk Harbor

Newhall House

Slaughterhouse Canyon

To Incline Village

To South Lake Tahoe

28

P
8

Kilometer   0   0.25

Mile   0   0.25

When you reach the trail junction with the road into Slaughterhouse Canyon, stay right (straight) on the broad road to Skunk Harbor. The route drops more steeply, rounding a switchback and passing through a clearing. Another switchback loops through woodland, then the trail narrows and enters a swampy area watered by an ephemeral stream.

Just beyond the moist patch, the trail forks. Go left (west) and meander down through lush undergrowth, crossing a streamlet, to the Newhall House. Footpaths lead around to the side of the house facing the lake and Skunk Harbor proper, with the pilings of a ruined dock stretching into the water. Explore the beach, then return as you came, keeping in mind that it's all uphill from here. It takes a bit longer to climb out than it does to descend.

Miles and Directions

0.0   Start by passing the green gate and heading down the broad access road.

0.4   Pass the junction with the trail that leads left (down and south) to Slaughterhouse Canyon. Stay right (down and west) on the road to Skunk Harbor.

1.0   Round a switchback.

1.4   Reach the T junction above the harbor. Beach access trails are to the right (north); Newhall House is to the left (south).

1.5   Arrive at the house and beach. Rest and relax at the waterside, then retrace your steps.

3.0   Arrive back at the trailhead.

9 Spooner Lake Loop

Once a water source for prospectors working silver mines near Virginia City, Spooner Lake is now the gateway to Lake Tahoe–Nevada State Park's Spooner Backcountry and is the centerpiece of a splendid short hike that circumnavigates its shoreline.

Start: Main parking lot for Lake Tahoe-Nevada State Park
Distance: 2.1-mile loop
Hiking time: About 1.5 hours
Difficulty: Easy
Trail surface: Singletrack, dirt roadway, pavement
Best seasons: Late spring, summer, fall (when the aspens turn)
Other trail users: None on the loop itself; cyclists on the portions leading to and from the loop
Trail amenities: Parking, restrooms, water, information, picnic areas. The park also hosts backcountry cabins, walk-in primitive camping, and backpacking, and superlative mountain biking.
Canine compatibility: Leashed dogs permitted
Fees and permits: Day-use fee
Schedule: Sunrise to sunset daily.
Maps: USGS Glenbrook NV; state park map available at the entrance station; information board map at the trailhead
Trail contact: Lake Tahoe–Nevada State Park, PO Box 6116, Incline Village, NV 89452; (775) 831-0494; http://parks.nv.gov/parks/lake-tahoe-nevada-state-park-1

Finding the trailhead: From the junction of NV 28 and Village Boulevard in Incline Village, follow NV 28 south for about 11 miles to the signed turnoff into Lake Tahoe–Nevada State Park. Turn left (east) into the park and follow the park road to the trailhead. From South Lake Tahoe/Stateline, follow US 50 north for about 12 miles to the junction with NV 28. Go left (west) onto NV 28 for 0.5 mile to the park entrance on the right. GPS: N39 06.369' / W119 54.963'

The Hike

Glades of quaking aspen, their chattering leaves bright green in spring and vivid gold in fall, crowd the first mile of this flat circuit around Spooner Lake. The aspen groves, some featuring gnarly old specimens with thick trunks scarred by graffiti, blend into an evergreen woodland on the lake's northern shores, with wildflowers sprinkled in meadow grasses flourishing in small clearings. Breaks in the trees allow views across the water, where ducks and other waterfowl swim and spotting an osprey is possible.

The large information sign at the trailhead—the first of a series of interpretive signs scattered along the loop—shows the extensive trail system that explores the backcountry surrounding Marlette Lake and Hobart Reservoir. Spooner Lake offers a sampling of what's found farther in. Interpretive signs also detail how the lake was integrated into the complex water and lumber delivery systems that fed resources from the Sierra to the silver mines in Nevada. An amazing array of railroads, haul roads, and flumes originating around Lake Tahoe carried water and timber to the mines, with Spooner Lake, then part of Spooner Ranch, strategically located near the east-side summit. The ranch owner, Michel Spooner, along with a partner, established Spooner Station in 1860, with a mill, hotel, saloon, and more accommodating the needs of miners, lumberjacks, and travelers.

From the trailhead follow the paved, interpretive Beetle Discovery Trail down through the picnic area; trailside interpretive signs detail the history of the lake, the wildlife and plant life it supports, and cross-country skiing opportunities. Follow the dirt road downhill to the junction with the

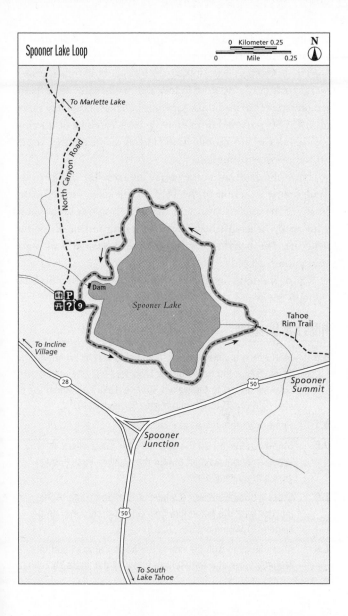

Spooner Lake Loop

0   Kilometer 0.25

0   Mile   0.25

N

To Marlette Lake

North Canyon Road

Dam

Spooner Lake

Tahoe
Rim Trail

To Incline
Village

28

50

Spooner
Summit

Spooner
Junction

50

To South
Lake Tahoe

Spooner Lake Trail. The loop begins here and is described in a counterclockwise direction.

The ecotones—meadow, aspen forest, coniferous forest— merge seamlessly as you follow the well-maintained path, which is accessorized with viewing benches. Highway noise from US 50, screened from view by trees, can be a distraction at first, but the automobile hum fades as you reach the woods on the northern shoreline.

Near the halfway point you'll intersect the Tahoe Rim Trail; follow a section of the TRT to the lake's earthen dam. Many of the anglers who visit the lake hang out at the dam, with rocky beaches suitable for picnicking just north of the structure. The bugs can be brutal here in season; walk with your mouth closed!

Close the loop on the far side of the dam by climbing through the woods to the parking area and trailhead.

Miles and Directions

0.0   Start at the trailhead next to the restrooms, signed for "All Trails." Follow the paved Beetle Discovery Trail, then head downhill on dirt to the signed Spooner Lake Trail, where you'll stay right (east) to circumnavigate Spooner Lake.

0.1   Head down through a meadow.

0.6   Stay left (straight) on the Spooner Lake Loop where an access trail breaks right toward the highway. Pass through groves of quaking aspen.

1.0   Cross a boardwalk over the inlet stream and climb to the junction with the Tahoe Rim Trail. Go left (northwest) on the signed TRT/Spooner Lake Loop.

1.6   At the junction with the link to the North Canyon Road to Marlette Lake, stay left (south), following the lake's shoreline.

1.8   Arrive at the dam and a trail junction. Cross the dam and
           then the gravel road to the sign that points uphill to the park-
           ing area. Two paths lead through the woods; pick one and
           start the short climb.

2.1   Arrive back at the trailhead.

Options: Miles of trails head north into the Marlette-
Hobart backcountry from the Spooner Lake trailhead. For
the hardier hiker, a fine 10-mile lollipop loop leads from
Spooner Lake to Marlette Lake and back. After a brief walk
along the aspen-lined North Canyon Road, which you'll
share with mountain bikers, a hikers-only trail breaks left and
traverses up past the remnants of an old woodcutter's cabin,
then on to Marlette Lake, which is big, blue, and inviting. You
can return as you came, or follow North Canyon Road back
down to the trailhead, forming a loop. The famous Flume
Trail can also be reached from the backcountry: A mountain
biker's favorite, this route doesn't see much foot traffic.

   The Tahoe Rim Trail also can be reached from nearby
Spooner Summit, located a short distance up NV 28 and
US 50 from the park entrance. From the summit the TRT
heads north to Snow Valley Peak and beyond; heading
south, it skirts Duane Bliss Peak and continues to Kingsbury
Grade and beyond. Walking north or south on the TRT
for 2 to 3 miles from the summit offers off-the-beaten-
path opportunities for the day hiker. While no summits
or peaks lie within a short hike's reach on the TRT, these
stretches of trail feature occasional vista points and make for
peaceful walks in the woods.

10 Five Lakes Trail

The surprise of summertime at a ski area reveals beauty through a different lens. The climb to Five Lakes offers access (not lift-served) to the slopes near Alpine Meadows, then mellows in the shady forest surrounding the first of the Five Lakes. Given the stiffness of the ascent and descent, this one pushes the boundaries of easy, but is worth the effort.

Start: Signed trailhead alongside Deer Park Drive
Distance: 4.2 miles out and back
Hiking time: 2–3 hours
Difficulty: More challenging due to 1,000-foot elevation gain. The trail is mostly shadeless and can be hot.
Trail surface: Dirt singletrack
Best seasons: Late spring, summer mornings, fall
Other trail users: None
Trail amenities: None
Canine compatibility: Dogs permitted except where posted in the Granite Chief Wilderness
Fees and permits: None
Schedule: Sunrise to sunset daily
Maps: USGS Tahoe City and Granite Chief CA; Lake Tahoe Basin Management Unit Map; National Geographic 803 Lake Tahoe Basin Trail Map
Trail contact: Tahoe National Forest, Truckee Ranger District, 10811 Stockrest Springs Rd., Truckee, CA 96161; (530) 587-3558; www.fs.usda.gov/tahoe. US Forest Service Lake Tahoe Basin Management Unit, Forest Supervisor's Office, 35 College Dr., South Lake Tahoe, CA 96150; (530) 543-2600; www.fs.usda.gov/ltbmu.
Special considerations: Given the elevation gain and exposure, do not attempt the hike if you have heart, respiratory, or knee problems.

Finding the trailhead: From the intersection of CA 89 and CA 28 in Tahoe City, follow CA 89 northwest (toward Truckee) for 3.6 miles.

Turn left (west) onto Alpine Meadows Road and go 2.2 miles to the trailhead, which is across from the second intersection with Deer Park Drive. Limited parking is available along Alpine Meadows Road. GPS: N39 10.749' / W120 13.790'

The Hike

Three distinct settings, and thus three distinct moods, lie along the trail to Five Lakes. The most arduous part of the trek is at the outset, where switchbacks climb through a sun-fed thicket of manzanita, mule ear, and snowberry. The second section features great views of the Alpine Meadows Ski Area, metal ski lift towers punched into smooth, colorful granite slabs, as well as an exposed traverse of a shallow granite-walled canyon. On the short third leg, a thick fir forest takes over, obscuring views and hiding all but one of the five small lakes that nestle in the shade.

As for the moods—well, the first pitch is just plain vexing, the second pitch revitalizes with great views, and the third is peaceful and contemplative.

Begin by climbing switchbacks . . . and more switchbacks . . . up the mountainside north of Bear Creek. Keep climbing until you leave the scrub behind; the terrain becomes more alpine as you ascend, and views open down-canyon toward the Truckee River valley and up-canyon onto the slopes of the Alpine Meadows Ski Area. Round another switchback, and then climb under ski lift towers into a saddle, where the trail enters a narrowing side canyon with black-streaked walls. Two switchbacks are built like giant stair steps into orange rock. Beyond, the route traverses above the canyon to more gentle switchbacks. At the outskirts of the fir forest, a sign denotes the boundary of the Granite Chief Wilderness.

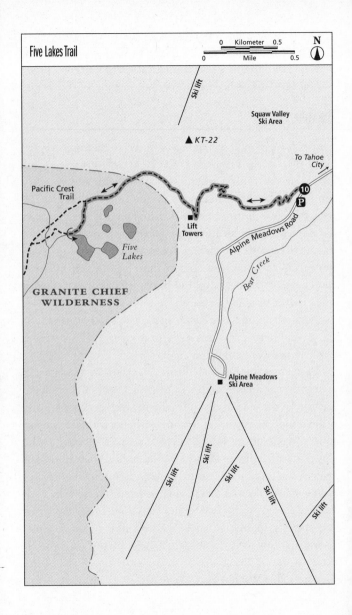

Five Lakes Trail

0　　Kilometer　0.5
0　　Mile　0.5

N

Squaw Valley
Ski Area

▲ KT-22

Ski lift

To Tahoe
City

Pacific Crest
Trail

10
P

Lift
Towers

Alpine Meadows Road

Five
Lakes

GRANITE CHIEF
WILDERNESS

Bear Creek

Alpine Meadows
Ski Area

Ski lift

Ski lift

Ski lift

Ski lift

Ski lift

Trails collide in the woods. At the signed junction with the Pacific Crest Trail (PCT), go left (south) to the shoreline of one of the small lakes, where social trails lead to inviting rest spots on the water. You'll have to bushwhack and do some clever off-trail navigating to find the other nearby lakes. Visit for a time, then return as you came.

Miles and Directions

0.0   Start at the "Granite Chief Wilderness" trail sign. It's all uphill from here, with switchbacks and granite stair steps aiding in the ascent. Take it slowly and enjoy the views.

1.1   Pass under ski area lift towers (you'll wish you could commandeer a chair by this point).

1.2   Cross a small saddle and curve into a granite-walled side canyon.

1.4   Negotiate switchbacks carved into orange rock.

1.7   Pass into the Granite Chief Wilderness.

2.0   At the signed junction of the Five Lakes Trail and the PCT to Whiskey Creek Camp, stay left (south).

2.1   Reach the shoreline of one of the Five Lakes. The others can't be seen. This is the turnaround point.

4.2   Arrive back at the trailhead.

Option: The trail continues through a meadow and on to a second junction with the PCT at 2.5 miles. From there you can hike or backpack to Whiskey Creek Camp and other destinations in the Granite Chief Wilderness.

11 Shirley Canyon Cascades

Squaw Creek rambles down a steep canyon from the heights of Granite Chief and Solitude to the Squaw Valley ski resort's busy village. A trail climbs more than 1,300 feet from the base to the top of the resort's aerial tram, but to keep it easy, this route takes you as far as a set of lovely cascades.

Start: Signed trailhead at the junction of Squaw Peak Road and Squaw Peak Way
Distance: 1.5 miles out and back (or more)
Hiking time: 1–2 hours
Difficulty: Moderate due to route-finding
Trail surface: Faint dirt and rock pathway
Best seasons: Late spring and early summer, when snowmelt fills the creek
Other trail users: None
Trail amenities: Information signboard
Canine compatibility: Leashed dogs permitted (though they often run off-leash)

Fees and permits: None
Schedule: Sunrise to sunset daily
Maps: USGS Tahoe City and Granite Chief CA; Lake Tahoe Basin Management Unit Map; National Geographic 803 Lake Tahoe Basin Trail Map
Trail contact: Squaw Valley Resort, 1960 Squaw Valley Rd./ PO Box 2007, Olympic Valley, CA 96146; (800) 403-0206; squawalpine.com. US Forest Service Lake Tahoe Basin Management Unit, Forest Supervisor's Office, 35 College Dr., South Lake Tahoe, CA 96150; (530) 543-2600; www.fs.usda.gov/ltbmu.

Finding the trailhead: From the intersection of CA 89 and CA 28 in Tahoe City, follow CA 89 northwest (toward Truckee) for 5 miles. Turn left (west) onto Squaw Valley Road and go 2.5 miles, past the huge village parking lot, to Squaw Peak Road. Turn right onto Squaw Peak

Road and follow it for 0.4 mile to its junction with Squaw Peak Way. Limited parking is available alongside both Squaw Peak Road and Squaw Peak Way. GPS: N39 11.910' / W120 14.480'

The Hike

The Squaw Valley resort is busy year-round. Its aerial tram runs daily, offering access to High Camp, with a pool, skating rink, restaurant and bar, and access to hiking trails that skim the high ridges overlooking the Truckee River valley and Tahoe basin.

But just beyond the bustling village at the base, the trail up Shirley Canyon offers a quiet change of pace. The path is rustic almost from the start: no wide, crushed gravel treadways or boardwalks to keep you on track. Instead, the singletrack climbs alongside Squaw Creek, which rocks and rolls in a meltwater rush in late spring and early summer. The destination is a small waterfall and a series of cascades that mist the trail and those who travel on it.

Begin by passing behind the large, obvious information signboard, which shows a map of the route. The trail is obvious at first, but grows indistinct as it meanders up into the steep-walled canyon. Watch for blue blazes on rocks, which show the way, and stay left of the creek. While the path unceasingly ascends, the real challenge is in picking the most comfortable and obvious way forward.

Pass a trail marker, then reach the first cascade/waterfall at 0.3 mile. You can turn around here or continue uphill to a second tumble. If you choose to continue, pass another trail marker and then bear left through the woods on a nice, straightforward stretch of trail along the left side of the creek. Where paths diverge at about 0.8 mile, stay left, then cross

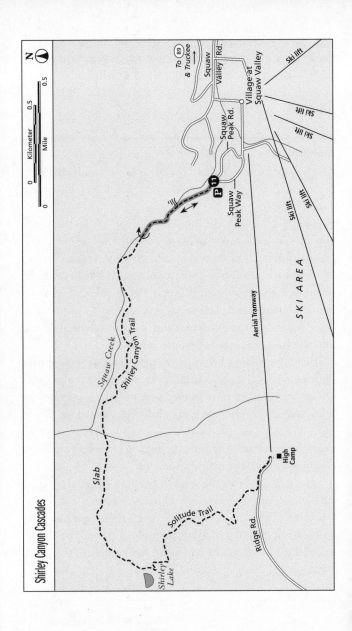

Shirley Canyon Cascades

N

Shirley Canyon Trail

Squaw Creek

Slab

Shirley Lake

Solitude Trail

Ridge Rd.

High Camp

Aerial Tramway

SKI AREA

Ski lift

Ski lift

Ski lift

Ski lift

Ski lift

Village at Squaw Valley

Squaw Peak Rd.

Squaw Valley Rd.

To 89 & Truckee

Squaw Peak Way

P 11

0   Kilometer   0.5

0   Mile   0.5

a granite slab (follow the blue blazes) to another cascade view. The trail continues upward and onward, but this is the turnaround point.

A preview of what lies ahead should you keep walking: The path leaves and then returns to the creek a final time before beginning to climb in earnest toward Shirley Lake and the Squaw Valley ski area's Solitude basin. If you make it up the crux of the route—an imposing granite headwall—you not only earn a lunch spot on the Shirley Lake shoreline but can also climb to the tram and then hitch a ride down.

Miles and Directions

0.0   Start at the Shirley Canyon trailhead. The route heads up the left side of the creek; where the trail becomes indistinct, look for blue blazes and trail markers.

0.3   Reach the waterfall. You can turn around here or continue to a second series of cascades.

0.5   Pass a trail marker, cross a side stream, then stay left on a straightforward path through the woods.

0.8   Where the paths diverge, stay left, cross a granite slab following blue blazes, and reach the second cascade view. Check it out, then return as you came.

1.5   Arrive back at the trailhead.

Option: Hardy hikers should not miss the climb to Shirley Lake and then to High Camp and a spectacular (and free) tram ride down to the base area of the Squaw Valley ski resort. From the second cascade continue uphill, following the blue blazes where the trail grows faint. Steep pitches are interspersed with relatively flat sections, leading up to a trail junction at 1.3 miles where signs point the way to Shirley Lake. At about the 2-mile mark, you'll encounter the headwall. Climb the steep, imposing slab on its left side, again following blue blazes and the occasional rock cairn. Top out and proceed through woodland to Shirley Lake and the Solitude basin (with ski lift) at 3.25 miles. The trail to High Camp climbs a rocky slope out of the basin (follow the Solitude/High Camp trail markers), then winds up the barren slopes to the broad roadway that links back to High Camp and the aerial tram. The views from on high are panoramic, with Lake Tahoe winking blue between the ridges. Total mileage to High Camp is just more than 4 miles.

12 Antone Meadows

This wander through the woods in a state park with few frills leads to a secluded meadow frequented by deer, ducks, and not a whole lot of humans.

Start: Unsigned road that leads straight west from the parking area

Distance: 6.1-mile loop

Hiking time: 3–4 hours

Difficulty: Moderate due only to length

Trail surface: Dirt roadway, singletrack

Best seasons: Late spring, summer, fall

Other trail users: Mountain bikers, trail runners

Trail amenities: A park sign with a map

Canine compatibility: Leashed dogs permitted on fire roads, but not in the natural preserve or on the trail at Antone Meadows

Fees and permits: None

Schedule: Sunrise to sunset daily

Maps: USGS Tahoe City CA; Burton Creek State Park brochure and map online

Trail contact: Burton Creek State Park; www.parks.ca.gov

Finding the trailhead: From the intersection of CA 89 and CA 28 in Tahoe City, follow CA 28 north for 1.6 miles to an unsigned left turn just before Tamarack Lodge. The left turn onto the Burton Creek State Park access road is almost directly opposite the road into Star Harbor. Follow the access road for 0.2 mile, staying left past Tamarack Lodge; the pavement is replaced by gravel after about 0.1 mile. Parking is in a clearing just beyond the park sign. GPS: N39 11.199' / W120 07.504'

The Hike

Burton Creek State Park, home to Antone Meadows and the preserve that protects it, is the shy sibling of the flashier state parks around Lake Tahoe. Come here for quiet; come here to retreat on a long, peaceful walk in the woods.

That said, you won't be entirely alone. The dirt roads crisscrossing through pine and fir are popular with mountain bikers. In my experience the cyclists, sometimes single and sometimes riding in packs, are friendly and easy to share the trails with. They come and go quickly, so you'll have the trails mostly to yourself even if you have a number of encounters.

Antone Meadows is a long stretch of flowing grasses and willow watered by Burton Creek, which meanders lazily down toward Lake Tahoe. It's a lovely spot and well worth the journey, but the journey is also the goal.

The loop begins by climbing via the dirt road that leads straight ahead (to the west) from the parking area. The steeper trail to the right (north) is the return route. After a brief uphill the road crosses a bridge spanning Burton Creek, then begins to climb again.

Pay attention to the numbers tacked onto the trees at the trail junctions; maps have been installed at these junctions as well to keep hikers, mountain bikers, and winter cross-country skiers on track. Pass a series of numbered intersections before you reach the signed singletrack trail that breaks left (west) toward Antone Meadows Natural Preserve.

The trail to the preserve is where the wandering begins— wandering mind and wandering shoes. The meadow remains out of sight until you reach its head. It dominates the right-hand side of the trail as you head east, back toward the lake. Watch the water for fowl; ducks and geese ply the shallow, curling creek.

The singletrack eventually dumps you back onto dirt roadways, which you'll follow back down to the trailhead. Views of the lake appear through the trees as you near trail's

Antone Meadows

end, and watch your step on the steep final descent to the parking area.

Miles and Directions

0.0   Start on the dirt road that heads straight west. The steeper trail to the right (north) is the return route.

0.2   Cross the bridge over Burton Creek.

0.4   Reach trail junction 15. Stay right.

1.4   At the trail Y (with no sign) stay right; just beyond is trail junction 12, with a trail map. Stay right again.

1.8   Reach the junction with the Antone Meadows Natural Preserve Trail (trail junction 11). Take the singletrack that breaks left, away from the road.

3.0   Reach trail junction 18 at the park boundary and the head of Antone Meadows. Cross a plank bridge over crystalline Burton Creek and begin heading east. The grassland, with the willow-lined creek, dominates the outset of the return leg of the loop.

4.3   Reach a five-way trail junction at junction 8; continue straight toward trail junction 7. A left turn leads into the Dollar Unit (an adjacent parcel of public land), and a right leads back to the roadway you traveled in on.

5.1   Reach trail junction 9 (also with a map). Continue straight, paralleling Burton Creek on the downhill run. Enjoy brief lake views between this junction and the next.

5.7   At trail junction 2 (a three-way intersection) stay right, heading downhill. The left turn heads toward North Tahoe High School.

5.9   Drop down steeply off the forested bench toward the trailhead.

6.1   Arrive back at the trailhead.

13 Truckee River Trail

One of the most visible and popular trails in north Lake Tahoe, this paved route parallels the Truckee River from Tahoe City to Alpine Meadows Road and beyond. Along its length you'll enjoy views of the sparkling river, the lush riparian habitat along the banks, the dark evergreen forest blanketing the valley walls, and the colorful crowds floating the river.

Start: Signed trailhead in 64-Acres Park at the Y in Tahoe City
Distance: 7.2 miles out and back
Hiking time: 4–5 hours
Difficulty: Moderate due only to length
Trail surface: Paved bike path
Best seasons: Spring, summer, fall
Other trail users: Lots of cyclists, runners, skaters
Trail amenities: Restrooms, interpretive signs. Porta-pottys are spaced along the trail.
Canine compatibility: Leashed dogs permitted
Fees and permits: None

Schedule: Sunrise to sunset daily
Maps: USGS Tahoe City CA; Lake Tahoe Basin Management Unit Map; National Geographic 803 Lake Tahoe Basin Trail Map; Tom Harrison Recreation Map of Lake Tahoe
Trail contact: Tahoe City Public Utility District, Parks and Recreation Department, 221 Fairway Dr., Tahoe City, CA 96145; (530) 583-3796; www.tcpud.com
Special considerations: The route is wheelchair accessible. Upgrades to the trail were under way in 2018.

Finding the trailhead: From the signalized intersection of CA 89 and CA 28 in Tahoe City, go 0.2 mile south on CA 89 to a signed right turn into the large trailhead parking area at 64-Acres Park. GPS: N39 09.866' / W120 08.866'

The Hike

On long, hot summer days, the Truckee River swirls with the revelry of river rafters. The clear water, a rich green fading to gold in the shallows, is topped by the dazzling blues, oranges, and yellows of the rafts, and the vibrant colors of boaters' swimsuits and hats. This riotous rainbow spills onto the trail that follows the river from Tahoe City to the inn at River Ranch, where neon-clad cyclists and runners mingle with families in denim and khaki and anglers in rubberized camouflage.

It is virtually impossible to get lost on the Truckee River Trail; if you wander into the water or find yourself sharing the asphalt with automobiles, you've strayed from the route. Mile markers are provided. A broken yellow line down the center separates downstream traffic from those headed upstream. Proximity to the highway precludes any illusion of this being a wilderness hike, but the route makes for an entertaining family outing, and is wheelchair accessible.

Begin by crossing the arcing bridge to the north shore of the river, then bear left (west), walking between the watercourse and CA 89. Passage around businesses and over driveways makes for an inauspicious start—and one that will change with a highway realignment underway when this guide went to press. But once the trail drops waterside, dense willow forms a buffer to the roadway and sometimes hides the meandering river. The only intersections, once you leave Tahoe City, are with the driveways and private bridges of lucky souls with homes perched on the riverbanks.

Sandbars in the river offer respite for the rafters; for hikers and other trail users, narrow social paths lead to small rocky or sandy beaches that serve as viewpoints, picnic spots, or rest and turnaround spots. Hike as far as you'd like; if you have

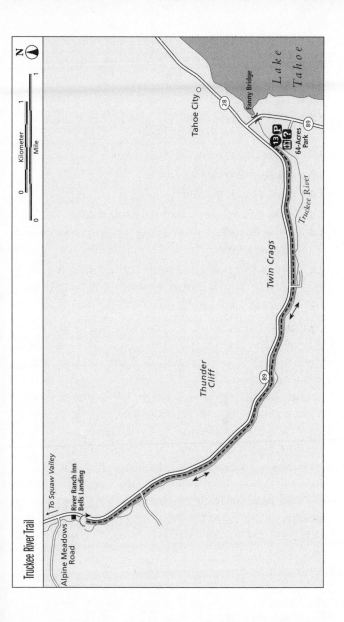

Truckee River Trail

N

Alpine Meadows
Road

To Squaw Valley

River Ranch Inn
Bells Landing

Thunder
Cliff

89

Twin Crags

Tahoe City ○

Fanny Bridge

28

89

13 P

2

64-Acres
Park

Truckee River

*Lake
Tahoe*

Kilometer

Mile

0   1

the time and energy, follow the trail all the way to Alpine Meadows Road and River Ranch. Return as you came.

Miles and Directions

0.0   Start by crossing the bridge in 64-Acres Park, then turn left (west) onto the paved bike path.

0.2   Leave the outskirts of Tahoe City behind.

1.0   Pass a mile marker.

2.0   Pass the next mile marker.

3.0   Pass the third mile marker and a private driveway.

3.4   Climb the only hill along the route (it's short) to the rafters' staging area.

3.6   Reach Bells Landing and the inn at River Ranch. Have a cool drink on the patio, then retrace your steps to the trailhead.

7.2   Arrive back at the trailhead.

Options: From River Ranch you can continue west on the Truckee River Trail to Squaw Valley Road. The total round-trip is 10 miles; maps are available at the Parks and Recreation Department office.

The Truckee River trailhead in Tahoe City also serves as the junction for other lakeshore bike paths, including the paved trail that heads north to Dollar Point, and one that follows CA 89 south to Sugar Pine Point State Park.

Finally, a nice section of the Tahoe Rim Trail (TRT) begins near downtown Tahoe City and leads about 2 miles to a vista point. To reach this part of the TRT from near the junction of CA 28 and CA 89, turn right onto Fairway Drive and go 0.2 mile to the parking lot at the Fairway Community Center.

14 Page Meadows

A favorite hike of Tahoe locals and visitors alike, Page Meadows hosts one of the best wildflower blooms in the basin. It greens up after the snow melts, sprouts a rainbow palette of blossoms by late June, and remains a restful, scenic destination through the rest of the hiking season. A steady climb on the Tahoe Rim Trail leads to the meadows.

Start: Ward Creek Boulevard. The trail is across the road (on the north side) from the trailhead signboard and creek.

Distance: 3.3 miles out and back

Hiking time: 2–2.5 hours

Difficulty: Moderate due to length and 400-foot elevation gain

Trail surface: Singletrack, logging road

Best seasons: Late spring and early summer for the wildflower bloom

Other trail users: Mountain bikers, equestrians, off-road vehicles on adjacent trails

Trail amenities: None

Canine compatibility: Dogs permitted

Fees and permits: None

Schedule: Dawn to dusk daily

Maps: USGS Tahoe City CA; Tahoe Rim Trail map for the Barker Pass to Tahoe City section available at the trailhead and online; National Geographic 803 Lake Tahoe Basin Trail Map

Trail contact: US Forest Service Lake Tahoe Basin Management Unit, Forest Supervisor's Office, 35 College Dr., South Lake Tahoe, CA 96150; (530) 543-2600; www.fs.usda.gov/ltbmu. Tahoe Rim Trail Association, 128 Market St., Ste. 3E/PO Box 3267, Stateline, NV 89449; (775) 298-4485; tahoerimtrail.org.

Finding the trailhead: From Tahoe City follow CA 89 south toward Homewood to Pineland Drive (with large "Pineland" signs). Turn right (west) onto Pineland Drive and go 0.3 mile to Twin Peaks Drive, where a sign points you toward "Ward Valley." Go left (south) onto Twin Peaks, then quickly right (west) onto Ward Creek Boulevard. Follow Ward Creek Boulevard for 1.5 miles to the signed TRT trailhead. Park alongside Ward Creek Boulevard. GPS: N39 08.435' / W120 11.522'

The Hike

In a typical high-country wildflower display, clusters of blooms erupt in patches among verdant meadow grasses. The blossoms of Page Meadows, situated above Ward Valley at nearly 7,000 feet, are no exception. The brilliant mule ears, with their bright yellow sunflower-like heads, and the tall white umbrellas of cow parsnip border on flamboyance. But most of the meadow flowers are brushed onto the landscape with a light touch. Early in the season, red Indian paintbrush, purple shooting star and lupine, scarlet larkspur, pink pussy paws, and meadow penstemon, among others, brighten the meadow. Later in the season, as the grasses go gold and the aspen begin to turn, white yarrow and purple and yellow asters (among others) come to the forefront.

Page Meadows, a popular destination that, luckily, is expansive enough to accommodate all comers, is surrounded by a thick evergreen forest with borders of aspens that have been sculpted into low tangles by heavy winter snowpacks. A network of trails explores the interlocking meadows; the treadways are raised using cement landscaping tiles, which allow passage without damaging the ecosystem—and help keep boots dry as well.

The section of the Tahoe Rim Trail that leads from Ward Creek to the meadows begins steeply, with the splashing of Ward Creek a pleasant accompaniment. At about the 0.5-mile mark, the climb mellows; pause to take in views of the craggy headwall of Ward Valley, where the architecture of the

Page Meadows

Kilometer 0.5
Mile 0.5

N

Tahoe Rim Trail

Page Meadows

Ward Creek Blvd

P 14

Ward Creek

To Tahoe City
& (89)

Granite Chief ridgetops, including Ward Peak and the backside of the Alpine Meadows ski area, is defined by snow well into June and early July.

Once on the crest the trail is intersected by access and OHV roads, but the route is clearly marked with the distinctive TRT trail markers (white on blue), as well as other signage. Follow the winding trail through the woods until the first meadow opens before you.

A narrow raised path cuts through the thick turf of the meadow, which is wet and may be snowy early in the season, with portions underwater—shallow vernal pools—into June. Side trails branch off to explore other parts of the meadow system. The bugs can be voracious, so wear long sleeves or douse yourself in repellent—otherwise, you may not be able to linger long enough to really get into the wildflower display.

The TRT bridges the main meadow and a smaller meadow through a narrow band of trees, then reenters the forest and rises to a sign noting the distances to the Ward Creek road and Tahoe City. This is the turnaround point. Return as you came to the trailhead.

Miles and Directions

0.0   Start on the north side of Ward Creek Boulevard; look for signs marking the TRT and describing backcountry camping regulations.

0.1   At the signed junction with a steep dirt roadway, go left (west) and uphill through the woods.

0.5   The climb mellows at a bend in the road, with views west to the head of Ward Valley.

0.7   Climb to a junction. Trail markers for the TRT, as well as for Page Meadows, are ahead. Stay left on the marked route, crossing two streamlets that may be dry in late season. The route narrows to singletrack.

1.1 Reach another trail not shown; stay right (northwest) on the signed TRT, passing low posts that prevent motor vehicle access.

1.2 Arrive at the first meadow.

1.5 Pass through a narrow band of trees to a second, smaller meadow.

1.7 Reach a TRT trail junction with a sign noting distances to the Ward Creek road and Tahoe City. Turn around here and retrace your steps.

3.3 Arrive back at the trailhead.

15 Ellis Peak Trail

Climbing onto the ridge above Blackwood Canyon is, without question, one of the more difficult undertakings in this guide. But the distance is short and the views from the top are a significant reward: Lake Tahoe lies broad and blue to the east, and the granite domes of the Desolation Wilderness shimmer to the west. Those with thighs of steel can continue to peaceful Ellis Lake.

Start: Signed trailhead at the summit of Barker Pass
Distance: 2.0 miles out and back
Hiking time: 1-2 hours
Difficulty: More challenging due to 800-foot climb to the ridge
Trail surface: Rocky singletrack
Best seasons: Summer, fall
Other trail users: The occasional hard-core mountain biker
Trail amenities: None
Canine compatibility: Leashed dogs permitted
Fees and permits: None
Schedule: Sunrise to sunset daily
Maps: USGS Homewood CA; Lake Tahoe Basin Management Unit Map; National Geographic 803 Lake Tahoe Basin Trail Map; Tom Harrison Recreation Map of Lake Tahoe

Trail contact: For the trail, contact the Tahoe National Forest, 10811 Stockrest Springs Rd., Truckee, CA 96161; (530) 587-3558; www.fs.usda.gov/tahoe. For trailhead access via Barker Pass Road, contact the US Forest Service Lake Tahoe Basin Management Unit, Forest Supervisor's Office, 35 College Dr., South Lake Tahoe, CA 96150; (530) 543-2600; www.fs.usda.gov/ltbmu.
Special considerations: Given the trail's steepness and elevation gain, do not attempt if you have heart, respiratory, or knee problems. The higher elevations of Barker Pass Road receive heavy winter snow, and the pass typically does not open until mid-June.

Finding the trailhead: From Tahoe City take CA 89 south for 4.1 miles to the turnoff marked for Kaspian and Blackwood Canyon. Turn right (west) onto Barker Pass Road. Stay left (south) where the road splits, crossing Blackwood Creek, and go about 7 miles to the signed trailhead on the left (west) side of the road just before the end of the pavement. Limited parking is available in pullouts along Barker Pass Road. GPS: N39 04.309' / W120 13.868'

The Hike

The splendor of the Sierran high country comes into perfect focus from a perch atop the rocky ridge crested by the Ellis Peak Trail. Cliffs drop sharply into the green valley of Blackwood Canyon, with Lake Tahoe a vast ink-blue stain on the gray and green landscape to the east. To the southwest lie the forbidding, gunmetal gray ramparts of the Desolation Wilderness, an impressive spread of flowing granite, lingering snowfields, and small, iridescent lakes.

Beyond this aerie, if you choose to go there, the mountains show another aspect of their makeup. Towering firs create a shady canopy overhead, and needles dense on the forest floor quiet the footfalls of hikers. The thunderhead-dark battlements of Ellis Peak rise above peaceful Ellis Lake, a pretty tarn in a classic alpine setting of evergreens and talus. The trek to the lake does not qualify as easy, but is worth the effort if time and fitness permit.

This hike begins with a relatively brutal climb up steep switchbacks. Views begin as you reach a ridgetop slope where broad-leaved mule's ear and other wildflowers hunker close to the ground, bowing to the weather. Tortured evergreens turn barren backsides to the prevailing west wind, forming a spindly windbreak as the route passes impressive rock outcrops that loom over Blackwood Canyon.

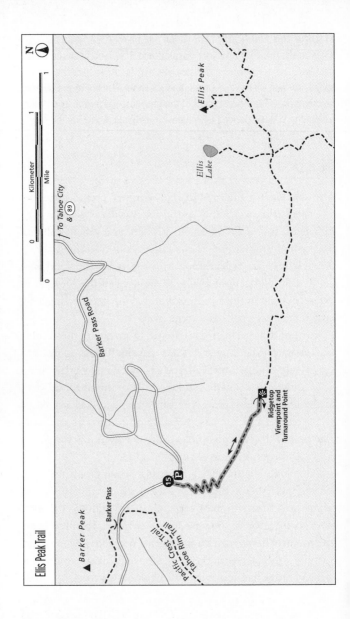

Ellis Peak Trail

N

Barker Peak ▲

Barker Pass

Pacific Crest Trail

Tahoe Rim Trail

Barker Pass Road

↑ To Tahoe City
& 89

15
P

Ridgetop Viewpoint and Turnaround Point

Ellis Lake

Ellis Peak ▲

Kilometer
Mile

Uninterrupted sunlight and tundra grasses blanket the high point, and wind-lashed trees hook over the trail. Look for a side trail leading left (east) onto a rock perch, where 360-degree views can be enjoyed. This is the turnaround point; return as you came.

Miles and Directions

0.0 Start by passing the trail sign and climbing steep switchbacks into the woods.

0.4 The climb eases as you reach a saddle with views of Lake Tahoe to the east, Loon Lake to the west, and the Desolation Wilderness to the southwest.

1.0 Follow the ridge up to where it mellows and offers viewpoints from overlook rocks. This is the turnaround point. If you continue, follow the obvious route south and east, which begins to drop into the woods and leads to Ellis Lake and Ellis Peak.

2.0 Arrive back at the trailhead.

Options: Beyond the overlook, the Ellis Peak Trail continues to Ellis Lake and the top of the namesake mountain. From the ridgetop the route descends into a forest of thick, lichen-coated firs. Skirt a meadow, then begin a gentle climb. The trail curls through a magnificent stand of old firs to a marked trail junction. To reach Ellis Lake (2.5 miles), go left on the gravel four-wheel-drive road, passing a shallow pond. The final stretch skirts a talus field that spills from the cliffs of Ellis Peak to bottle-green Ellis Lake. A mixed fir forest circles three-quarters of the lake, but on the south shore a steep spill of talus pours into the water.

To reach the summit of Ellis Peak, stay right at the signed trail junction and climb to the 8,688-foot summit. Once you've rested and refueled, return as you came. Plan on 3 to

4 hours of hiking (5–6 miles round-trip) to reach the lake and/or the peak.

You can enjoy another easy high-country ramble by traveling 0.5 mile west of the Ellis Peak trailhead on Barker Pass Road to the trailhead for the Pacific Crest and Tahoe Rim Trails (PCT/TRT). A 3-mile out-and-back hike heading north on the PCT/TRT offers a sampling of the rigors and beauty of the national scenic trail. Rugged but well maintained, user-friendly but not overcrowded, this stretch of trail offers wonderful views of Blackwood Canyon, Lake Tahoe, and the Desolation Wilderness. A plug of dark volcanic rock jutting from rose-colored earth marks the end of this recommended route, though you can follow the PCT all the way to Canada if you choose.

Following the TRT/PCT south leads gently down through interspersed clearings and open woodlands; again, hike as far as you choose (even all the way to Mexico). Richardson Lake is a nice destination for a long, upside-down hike, and the Desolation Wilderness boundary lies beyond.

16 General Creek Loop

Walk in the footsteps (or ski tracks) of Olympic biathletes along this woodland loop, which follows General Creek into Sugar Pine Point State Park's backcountry.

Start: Day-use trailhead in the parking lot for the Sugar Pine Point State Park amphitheater
Distance: 4.7-mile lollipop
Hiking time: 3–3.5 hours
Difficulty: Moderate
Trail surface: Dirt forest roads, paved road
Best seasons: Spring, summer, fall
Other trail users: Mountain bikers, trail runners
Trail amenities: Restrooms, water, camping, and information are available in the campground.
Canine compatibility: Leashed dogs permitted on the park roads
Fees and permits: Day-use fee

Schedule: The Sugar Pine Point State Park trail system is open for year-round recreation from sunrise to sunset daily. Entrance station hours vary; in summer it is open from about 8 a.m. until 8 p.m. daily.
Maps: USGS Homewood and Meeks Bay CA; map in the Sugar Pine Point State Park brochure, available at the campground entrance station and online
Trail contact: Ed Z'berg Sugar Pine Point State Park, Tahoma, CA; (530) 525-7982; www.parks .ca.gov

Finding the trailhead: From the Y junction of US 50 and CA 89 in South Lake Tahoe, follow CA 89 north for 17.5 miles to the signed entrance for Sugar Pine Point State Park. From the Y junction of CA 89 and CA 28 in Tahoe City, follow CA 89 south for 9.2 miles to the campground entrance. Proceed past the campground entrance station on the west side of the highway to parking for the campground amphitheater and the day-use trailhead. GPS (day-use trailhead): N39 03.38' / W120 07.287'

The Hike

The General Creek Loop follows part of the route biathletes traversed in the 1960 Squaw Valley Olympic Games, offering hikers a chance to gain a new appreciation for (or sense of astonishment at) one of the oddest sporting events ever conceived. In the biathlon, cross-country skiing—exhausting even when you are not racing—is paired with marksmanship; speed and accuracy determine the winner. Interpretive signs provide an introduction to the Nordic trail system established for the games, but the sign near the second bridge crossing General Creek, more than 2 miles into the woods, is an eye-opener. The pictures say it all: skiers sprawled belly-down in the snow with the rifles they've carried on their backs aimed at targets across the white meadow. Powerful imagery that's hard to grasp on a sunny summer's day.

This hike begins in the Sugar Pine Point State Park's campground. The most direct route to the trailhead proper is to follow the main campground road to the westernmost campground loop; the signed trail begins between campsites 147 and 149. A walking path skirts the campground to the south and is a nice option if you prefer to avoid pavement. An accessible campground path also leads to the westernmost camp loop.

From the camp follow the dirt fire road through the woodland. Pass a side trail that breaks left (south) into the campground, staying on the wide dirt track to the start of the loop portion of the route. Go left (south) to the first General Creek crossing; a bridge spans the waterway. On the opposite (south) side of the creek, go right (west) on the gently climbing track.

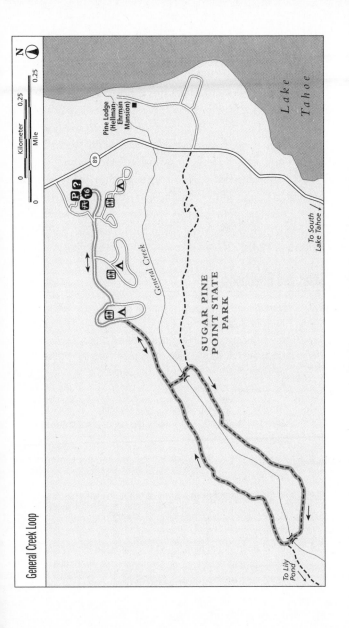

General Creek Loop

N

0   Kilometer   0.25

0   Mile   0.25

89

P ?
🥾 16
🚻
⛺

🚻 ⛺

🚻 ⛺

Pine Lodge
(Hellman-
Ehrman Mansion)

General Creek

SUGAR PINE
POINT STATE
PARK

To Lily
Pond

To South
Lake Tahoe

Lake
Tahoe

Follow the creek westward for a meditative mile through the quiet forest and a burned area where the undergrowth is thick and lush. Bend north past the biathlon sign to the second General Creek crossing. On the north side of the bridge, the singletrack Lily Pond Trail heads left (west). Stay right on the broad General Creek Loop, which follows the north side of the creek through an old burn where wildflowers, thimbleberries, and ferns flourish in spring and early summer.

Pass an unmarked junction with another dirt road on the descent, staying right (east). The trail/road drops to close the loop; from that point retrace your steps to the campground trailhead, then through the camp to the day-use parking lot and trail's end.

Miles and Directions

0.0 Start in the day-use/amphitheater parking lot, passing behind the closed gate on the paved roadway. Ski trail and nature trail signs mark a convergence of paved paths. Stay right on the paved trail to the main camp road, then go left (west) on the camp road. An accessible campground path also leads to the trailhead proper.

0.9 Arrive at the signed General Creek trailhead, between campsites 147 and 149. Head down the wide, graded dirt road into the woods.

1.0 Pass a side trail that leads left (south) into the campground. Stay straight on the main trail.

1.4 At the trail junction (the start of the loop) go left. Cross the bridge over the creek. At the trail intersection on the south bank, turn right (west).

2.4 At the head of the loop, cross the creek via the bridge. The Lily Pond Trail heads left on the far side of the bridge; stay right (east) on the General Creek trail.

3.1 At the unsigned junction with a dirt road, stay right (east).

3.4 Close the loop. Retrace your steps to the campground trailhead.

4.7 Arrive back at the amphitheater parking area.

Options: Sugar Pine Point offers a number of easy day hike options, including the Lakefront Interpretive Trail, the Ron Beaudry Trail, the Dolder Nature Trail, and the trail to Lily Pond. A few of the trails wind through the Edwin L. Z'berg National Preserve, named for the California state assemblyman who championed preservation and restoration efforts, and whose name was added to the park in 2004. Cap your visit to the state park with a tour of Pine Lodge (the Hellman-Ehrman mansion), an impressive 11,000-square-foot residence built as a retreat by banker Isaias Hellman.

17 The Lighthouse and Rubicon Point

High points along this loop in D. L. Bliss State Park have nothing to do with elevation gain. First there's the historic lighthouse on Rubicon Point, which offers panoramic views across Lake Tahoe. Another perk: an exposed stretch of trail that skims a rocky cliff far above the waterline.

Start: Signed trailhead alongside the park road 1 mile from the entrance station
Distance: 2.5-mile loop
Hiking time: About 2 hours
Difficulty: Moderate due to elevation changes
Trail surface: Dirt singletrack, rock staircases
Best seasons: Late spring, summer, fall
Other trail users: None
Trail amenities: Restrooms, information, and picnic facilities are available in the park.
Canine compatibility: Leashed dogs permitted in campgrounds, picnic areas, and on paved park roads. No dogs are permitted on the trails or beaches.
Fees and permits: Day-use fee
Schedule: The trail is available sunrise to sunset daily; visitor center hours vary, typically from 11 a.m. to 4 p.m. daily. If the entrance station is closed, use the self-pay registration envelopes.
Maps: USGS Emerald Bay CA; map provided in the D. L. Bliss State Park brochure
Trail contact: D. L. Bliss State Park, Tahoma, CA 96142; (530) 525-7277; www.parks.ca.gov

Finding the trailhead: From the intersection of US 50 and CA 89 in South Lake Tahoe, head north on CA 89 for 12.5 miles to the signed turnoff for D. L. Bliss State Park on the right (east). From Tahoe City, take CA 89 south for 15.8 miles to the park entrance. Follow the park road 1 mile east to the trailhead, which is on the left (west) side of the road. A limited number of visitors are admitted into the park; if you arrive after 10 a.m., check at the visitor center or entrance station for availability. GPS: N38 59.353' / W120 05.915'

The Hike

The historic lighthouse that once warned sailors on Lake Tahoe of submerged dangers off Rubicon Point is unassuming—it resembles, of all the unfortunate possibilities, a wooden outhouse. But in the early days of the twentieth century, the humble structure housed a brilliant acetylene light that was integral to navigation on the lake. The light no longer steers boaters clear of the hazardous shoreline, but the lighthouse, rebuilt in 2001, makes an interesting first stop along this loop in D. L. Bliss State Park.

The lighthouse isn't the only unique man-made artifact along this route. Climbing away from Calawee Cove, the trail is etched into a steep rocky face high above the lake. A rustic railing protects the cliff side of the path, but it doesn't mitigate the thrilling exposure or impede the superlative views. *A word of caution:* This stretch is not for those afraid of heights, and children should be watched carefully.

The Lighthouse Trail begins by climbing through a fire-scarred woodland. It flattens atop a ridge amid evergreens and boulders, then drops through more hauntingly beautiful burned forest. Drop to a trail junction with great views. The granite staircase leading to the lighthouse descends steeply to the small structure perched on a rocky shelf overlooking the lake.

Climb back to the trail crossing and go right (north) on the Lighthouse Trail, which follows long, shaded switchbacks down to the paved parking area at Calawee Cove. The cove's little beach is below the lot; the signed junction with the Rubicon Trail is to the right (south). Pick up the Rubicon and head up around the namesake point.

This is the exposed stretch: The rail protects against the abrupt lakeside drop, boardwalks span clefts in the cliff face,

The Lighthouse and Rubicon Point

0   Kilometer   0.5

0   Mile   0.5

N

Lake Tahoe

Lester Beach

Calawee Cove Beach

Rubicon Point

Rubicon Creek

To Tahoe City

Lighthouse Trail

Rubicon Trail

D. L. BLISS STATE PARK

P 17

89

Park Road

Park Entrance and Headquarters

To South Lake Tahoe

To Emerald Bay State Park

and head-thumping overhangs loom over the trail. It's so invigorating you might forget you are climbing . . . until you reach the granite staircase that ascends past a trail leading to the lighthouse. Stay left (south) on the Rubicon Trail, enjoying heavenly views as the trail flattens.

As you near the end of the loop, the trail curves away from the lake into dense forest. At the signed trail junction in a clearing, take the trail to the right (northwest); the left-hand trail leads south to Emerald Bay and Vikingsholm. The needle-carpeted path leads to the park road and closes the loop at the Lighthouse trailhead.

Miles and Directions

0.0   Start on the signed Lighthouse trailhead, crossing a small bridge and climbing into a burned woodland.

0.7   Drop to a trail intersection. Go left for about 10 feet to an interpretive sign and the top of the stone staircase leading down to the lighthouse. Descend the stairs.

0.8   Arrive at the lighthouse. Check it out, then climb back to the Lighthouse Trail and turn right (north).

1.4   Drop through the woods to the parking lot and restrooms at Calawee Cove. Pick up the signed Rubicon Trail and head right (south).

1.6   Reach the exposed part of the trail, with the wire rail protecting the cliff side and great views across the lake.

1.8   Climb a granite staircase past the trail to the lighthouse, staying left (south) on the Rubicon Trail.

2.1   Pass a trailside overlook.

2.4   Reach a clearing and trail junction. Go right (northwest) to the park road and trailhead.

2.5   Arrive back at the trailhead.

18 Vikingsholm and Emerald Point

Blue–green and opalescent, it's obvious how Tahoe's Emerald Bay earned its name. Spectacular Vikingsholm, at the head of the bay, is the obvious destination for most hikers. Not so obvious is the jewel of a trail that leads along the northern shoreline to the bay's narrow mouth.

Start: Emerald Bay State Park parking lot off CA 89; the signed trailhead is to the left of the huge rock slab overlooking the bay.

Distance: 5.2 miles out and back

Hiking time: 3–4 hours

Difficulty: Moderate due to elevation change and trail length

Trail surface: Graded dirt road, pavement, dirt singletrack

Best seasons: Spring, summer, fall

Other trail users: None

Trail amenities: A gift and information station in the parking lot; restrooms, a visitor center, and picnic facilities at Vikingsholm

Canine compatibility: No dogs are permitted on trails or beaches, or at Vikingsholm. Leashed dogs are permitted in the Eagle Point Campground.

Fees and permits: Parking fee

Schedule: The trail is open from sunrise to sunset daily. Vikings-holm and the Emerald Bay State Park visitor center are open from 10 a.m. to 4 p.m. daily Memorial Day to Labor Day, with limited hours earlier in May and later in Sept. Tours of Vikingsholm are available for a fee; call (530) 541-6498.

Maps: USGS Emerald Bay CA; Emerald Bay park map and brochure available online and at the visitor center

Trail contact: Emerald Bay State Park, Tahoma, CA 96142; (530) 541-3030 (summer only); www .parks.ca.gov

Special considerations: The highway and parking lots at Vikings-holm and neighboring Eagle Falls are congested during high season. Lots fill quickly, with additional parking available along the roadway. Please be courteous and safe in selecting a parking space.

Hikers must negotiate a 400-foot change in elevation within the first mile. Heed the trailhead sign that warns not to attempt the route if you have heart, respiratory, or knee problems.

Finding the trailhead: From the intersection of US 50 and CA 89 in South Lake Tahoe, head north on CA 89 for 10.7 miles to the large Emerald Bay State Park parking area on the right (southeast). From Tahoe City, take CA 89 south for 17.6 miles (parking is on the left). GPS: N38 57.261' / W120 06.619'

The Hike

Vikingsholm is arguably the most spectacular of all Lake Tahoe's shoreline estates, with striking Scandinavian architecture and views that open onto sparkling Emerald Bay. Lora Josephine Knight had the home built in 1929; she also commissioned construction of the little castle-like teahouse on the summit of Fannette Island—Lake Tahoe's only island, and, in the late 1880s, home of Captain Dick Barter, "the Hermit of Emerald Bay." The mansion, designed by architect Lennart Palme, Mrs. Knight's nephew, features huge carved timbers, massive native granite boulders mortared into exterior walls, and a sod roof sown with wildflowers.

Hiking down to visit the storied estate is a quintessential and massively popular Tahoe excursion. But stretch a bit beyond the estate along the Rubicon Trail and you can enjoy Emerald Bay in relative solitude. Walk quietly and watchfully as you near Emerald Point; you may see an eagle or osprey return to a lakeside nest, a tangle of twigs and branches perched at the top of a standing dead tree.

Begin by heading down the wide path (a human highway in the busy summer season) to Vikingsholm. Two

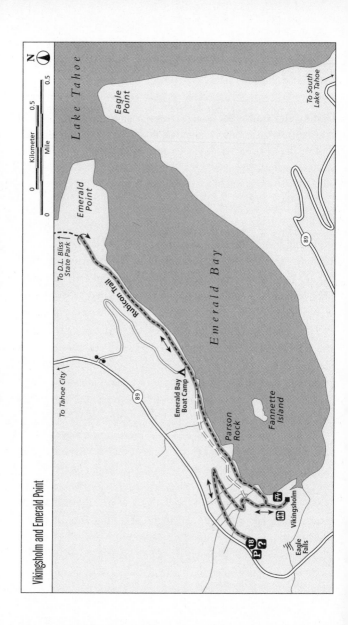

Vikingsholm and Emerald Point

switchbacks separated by long traverses drop to a junction, where a park map points you downhill and right through open woodland to Vikingsholm. Take some time to explore the grounds, check out the visitor center, take a tour of the house, and picnic on the beach. When you're ready to move on, pick up the signed Rubicon Trail on the northeast side of the main house (the right side as you stand on the beach facing the building).

A series of bridges and boardwalks assist passage along the forested shoreline trail, which is intersected by drainages and lush with berries, ferns, and other verdant undergrowth. It's easy going to Parson Rock, which overlooks the bay and Fannette Island just before the trail enters the Emerald Bay Boat Camp Campground.

The Rubicon Trail merges with the camp road for a stretch, then breaks back to the shoreline as a dirt path at a trail sign. The easy rambling continues, with short timber stairs leading down to half-moon beaches along the waterline. The mouth of the bay, pinched by Emerald Point on the north and Eagle Point on the south, remains in sight until the Rubicon begins to bend north toward Rubicon Bay and Calawee Cove. A clearing just before the trail heads north is the turnaround point (though any of the little beaches would work just as well). Return as you came, enjoying sporadic views up into the stony Desolation Wilderness as you go.

Miles and Directions

Note: Mileages include a 0.3-mile tour of the paved paths around Vikingsholm.

0.0   Start by descending the broad, well-graded trail.

1.0   Arrive at Vikingsholm and tour the grounds.

1.3	A signed trailhead for the Rubicon Trail is to the right (northeast) of Vikingsholm as you face it. Turn right (east) onto the flat path.
1.9	Enter the Emerald Bay Boat Camp and follow the paved road through the campsites.
2.1	At the east end of the camp, the signed Rubicon Trail breaks to the right (east), turning to dirt and following the shoreline.
2.4	Pass a series of short staircases that lead down to tiny beaches.
2.6	Reach a clearing near the tip of Emerald Point, with the obvious Rubicon Trail breaking left (north). This is the turnaround point. The social tracks dead-end in the brush. Retrace your steps back toward the trailhead.
5.2	Arrive back at the trailhead.

Option: The Rubicon Trail continues through neighboring D. L. Bliss State Park to Rubicon Point, a 4.5-mile one-way journey from Vikingsholm.

19 Eagle Lake

Dark and clear, Eagle Lake pools in a basin bordered by steep talus slopes and black-streaked rock walls. The lake's classic high Sierra setting makes it one of the most popular destinations around Lake Tahoe.

Start: Signed trailhead near the restrooms in the Eagle Falls parking lot
Distance: 2.0 miles out and back
Hiking time: About 1 hour
Difficulty: Moderate due to some steep climbing
Trail surface: Dirt singletrack, granite stairs
Best seasons: Summer, fall
Other trail users: None
Trail amenities: Restrooms, picnic sites
Canine compatibility: Leashed dogs permitted. Because the trail is so popular, owners are asked to keep their pets under control and to clean up any messes.
Fees and permits: Per-vehicle parking fee, if you can find space in the lot. Parking along CA 89 is free. A free wilderness permit, available at the trailhead, is required.
Schedule: Sunrise to sunset daily

Maps: USGS Emerald Bay CA; Lake Tahoe Basin Management Unit Map; National Geographic 803 Lake Tahoe Basin Trail Map; Tom Harrison's Recreation Map of Lake Tahoe
Trail contact: US Forest Service Lake Tahoe Basin Management Unit, Forest Supervisor's Office, 35 College Dr., South Lake Tahoe, CA 96150; (530) 543-2600; www.fs.usda.gov/ltbmu
Special considerations: The highway and parking lots at Eagle Falls and neighboring Vikingsholm are congested during the high season. Lots fill quickly, with additional parking available along the highway. Please be courteous and safe in selecting a parking space.

You will gain and lose about 400 feet in elevation and must climb and descend a stretch of granite steps, so be prepared for a moderate workout.

Finding the trailhead: From the intersection of US 50 and CA 89 in South Lake Tahoe, head north on CA 89 for 10.3 miles to the signed Eagle Falls parking area on the left (west). From Tahoe City follow CA 89 south for 18 miles, past the parking area for Vikingsholm, to the Eagle Falls parking lot on the right. GPS: N38 57.118' / W120 06.811'

The Hike

Eagle Lake is cupped within a stark Desolation Wilderness cirque; steep-walled, silver and gray, and formidable. The trail leading up to the lake is moderately challenging but quite short, making it well within reach of any hiker seeking an alpine experience without excess effort. Though not recommended, I've even seen hikers make the ascent in strappy sandals and flip-flops.

After filling out a wilderness permit, begin by climbing the stairs behind the trailhead sign, staying on the signed Eagle Lake Trail where it connects with the short loop to Upper Eagle Falls. The path climbs gently at first, allowing you to enjoy views of the cascade above Eagle Falls, and the pinnacles and great gray domes of the Desolation Wilderness.

Nearing the cascade, a twisting stone stairway leads up, then down, to a vista point and then the sturdy bridge spanning the cataract. Cross the bridge, then climb granite stairs and rocky singletrack past the wilderness boundary sign and up to a large, smooth granite slab dotted with pine and cedar. The trail is worn into the slab; rocks line the track as well.

The trail skirts a rock outcrop overlooking the lush creek bed below, then traverses above the drainage through the woods, with the jagged crowns of the canyon walls rising above the canopy. Gentle climbing takes you to a trail junction at 0.9 mile; from here you can head deeper into the

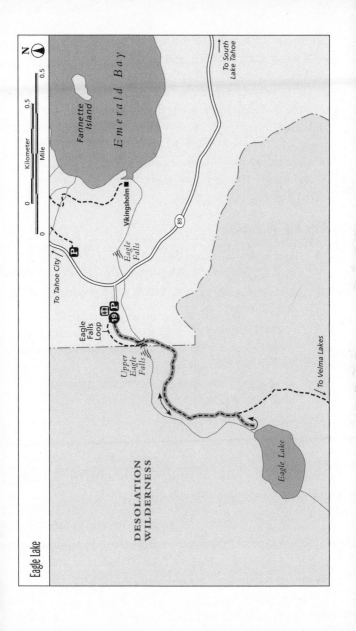

Eagle Lake

Desolation Wilderness, to the Velma Lakes and beyond. To reach Eagle Lake, however, bear right into the cirque.

Reach the shores of Eagle Lake at the 1-mile mark. A sprinkling of cedar, ponderosa, and Jeffrey pine provide shade from the vivid alpine sunshine. If you don't mind icy water, Eagle Lake invites a dip. There is no beach, however, so you'll have to dry off and/or enjoy the stunning views from a perch on a tree stump or a sunbaked granite slab.

Return the way you came, enjoying views of Lake Tahoe on the descent.

Miles and Directions

0.0 Start by climbing steps to the junction of the Eagle Lake Trail and the Eagle Falls Loop. Stay left (southwest) on the Eagle Lake Trail.

0.2 Climb granite steps past the second loop trail junction and stay left, crossing the bridge.

0.4 Enter the Desolation Wilderness.

0.9 At the junction with the trail to the Velma Lakes, stay right on the signed trail to Eagle Lake.

1.0 Arrive at Eagle Lake. Enjoy the scenery, then retrace your steps to the trailhead.

2.0 Arrive back at the trailhead.

Options: The trail intersection at Eagle Lake is but one gateway into the backcountry wonderland that is Desolation Wilderness. The nearest destinations are the Velma Lakes, reached via a grueling climb to more than 8,000 feet, then a lovely cruise across glacier-polished granite benches through sparse forest. The Velmas are almost 5 miles from the Eagle Falls trailhead, but the wilderness offers an abundance of hiking destinations, including Lake Aloha, Susie Lake, and Fontanillis Lake, as well as numerous backpacking options.

20 Cascade Falls

Though the falls cascade out of sight at trail's end, the views of Cascade Lake and Lake Tahoe from smooth granite slabs above the spill crown this moderate trek.

Start: Signed trailhead in Bayview Campground
Distance: 2.0 miles out and back
Hiking time: About 1.5 hours
Difficulty: Moderate due to climbs and descents over rocky terrain
Trail surface: Dirt and rocky singletrack, granite slabs
Best seasons: Late spring through midsummer, when snowmelt swells the falls
Other trail users: None
Trail amenities: Restrooms and information signboards in the campground
Canine compatibility: Leashed dogs permitted

Fees and permits: None
Schedule: Sunrise to sunset daily
Maps: USGS Emerald Bay CA; Lake Tahoe Basin Management Unit Map; National Geographic 803 Lake Tahoe Basin Trail Map; Tom Harrison Recreation Map of Lake Tahoe
Trail contact: US Forest Service Lake Tahoe Basin Management Unit, Forest Supervisor's Office, 35 College Dr., South Lake Tahoe, CA 96150; (530) 543-2600; www.fs.usda.gov/ltbmu
Other: Though the total elevation change is only about 80 feet, the trail traverses some steep, rocky terrain.

Finding the trailhead: From the intersection of US 50 and CA 89 in South Lake Tahoe, head north on CA 89 for 9.4 miles to a left (south) turn into the Bayview Campground. From Tahoe City follow CA 89 south for 18.9 miles, past the parking areas for Vikingsholm and Eagle Falls, to a right turn into the campground. Follow the campground road 0.3 mile to limited parking at the signed trailhead. Direct access to the trailhead may be difficult in high season; be prepared

to park outside the campground in safe pullouts along the highway.
GPS: N38 56.607' / W120 06.000'

The Hike

Though not in view until the end of the trail, boisterous Cascade Creek spills out of the high country to fuel Cascade Falls and fill secluded Cascade Lake. The dark, still lake, cupped in a wooded bowl and surrounded by private property, is off-limits to hikers. The falls are off-limits too, rendered inaccessible by steep granite faces. But hikers can chill their feet in pools and riffles above the plunge as the stream courses over and among smooth granite slabs. A seat at trail's end on a platform of sunbaked granite affords great vistas beyond the Cascade Lake basin to Lake Tahoe.

To begin, walk behind the information kiosk and turn left (south) onto the Cascade Trail. The path bends through mixed evergreen forest, then climbs a short stone stairway to overlook the falls, Cascade Lake, and the southern reaches of Lake Tahoe beyond.

At about the 0.5-mile mark, begin a rocky downward traverse of the slope on the northwest end of Cascade Lake. Pick your way along the base of a granite cliff, taking care as the footing is uneven. You can catch glimpses of the falls tumbling toward the lake, but make sure you stop before you look.

Cross a relatively narrow ledge, then climb granite steps and broken rock to the broad, sun-splashed slabs that cradle the creek. A lovely granite bowl opens upstream, stretching back into the Desolation Wilderness. A maze of trails has been worked onto the landscape over the years, some marked by "ducks" (stacks of rocks also called cairns), and others delineated by lines of rocks. Look left and downhill

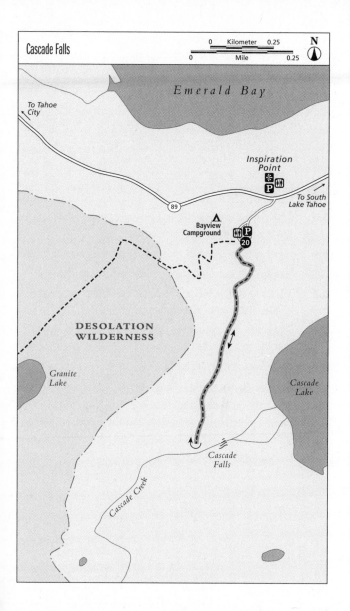

Cascade Falls

Emerald Bay

To Tahoe
City

Inspiration
Point

89

To South
Lake Tahoe

Bayview
Campground

20

DESOLATION
WILDERNESS

Granite
Lake

Cascade
Lake

Cascade
Falls

Cascade Creek

for a wooden trail marker that points the way to the falls overlook. Stay low (left and north) to get closer to the falls, but don't get too close as you don't want to risk a slip near the cliff face. Stay high (right) to reach stretches of the creek that permit water play and toe dipping.

The whole terrace opens on wonderful views across the southern Tahoe basin. Take in the sights, then return as you came.

Miles and Directions

0.0   Start behind the information signboard, turning left (south) at the sign on the trail to Cascade Falls.

0.5   Head up the stone steps to views of Cascade Lake and its falls.

0.7   Traverse via slabs and steps at the base of a granite wall.

0.8   The trail levels as you approach the creek, and the granite cirque opens uphill to the south.

1.0   Reach the creek above the falls. Enjoy the sun and views, then return as you came.

2.0   Arrive back at the trailhead.

Option: A right (southwest) turn at the trailhead puts you on the trail to Granite Lake in the Desolation Wilderness. A wilderness permit for day use is required and available at the trailhead.

21 Cathedral Lake

Iconic Mount Tallac, which dominates nearly every South Lake Tahoe vista, is a powerful presence on this hike. Cathedral Lake, a peaceful tarn cupped in jumbled rock and thick-trunked evergreens, lies at the terminus of one of the 9,738-foot peak's talus fields.

Start: Mount Tallac trailhead off CA 89 near Camp Shelly

Distance: 5.6 miles out and back

Hiking time: 4–5 hours

Difficulty: More challenging due to 1,100-foot elevation change

Trail surface: Dirt singletrack

Best seasons: Summer, early fall

Other trail users: None

Trail amenities: Information signboard

Canine compatibility: Leashed dogs permitted

Fees and permits: A free wilderness permit is required and available at the trailhead.

Schedule: 24 hours a day, 7 days a week, year-round

Maps: USGS Emerald Bay CA; Lake Tahoe Basin Management Unit Map; National Geographic 803 Lake Tahoe Basin Trail Map; Tom Harrison Recreation Map of Lake Tahoe

Trail contact: US Forest Service Lake Tahoe Basin Management Unit, Forest Supervisor's Office, 35 College Dr., South Lake Tahoe, CA 96150; (530) 543-2600; www.fs.usda.gov/ltbmu

Special considerations: Consider an easier hike if you have heart, respiratory, or knee problems.

Finding the trailhead: From the intersection of US 50 and CA 89 in South Lake Tahoe, head north on CA 89 for 4.1 miles to the turnoff for Camp Shelly and the Mount Tallac trailhead. Turn left onto the trailhead road and drive 0.4 mile to the first fork in the road, signed for the Mount Tallac trailhead and Camp Concord. Go left for 0.2 mile to another intersection. Stay straight (right) on FR 1306, again signed

for the Mount Tallac trailhead. The parking area is 0.5 mile ahead.
GPS: N38 55.283' / W120 04.086'

The Hike

The daunting ramparts of Mount Tallac shadow every foot
of the trail to Cathedral Lake. Though the elevation gain is
significant, the climbing is never painfully steep, and it's mit-
igated by great views, shade, and a stop to rest and refuel (or
turn around) at Floating Island Lake. The ultimate destination is Cathedral Lake, set in a talus-rimmed bowl near tree
line on Tallac's southeast flank.

Begin by climbing the narrow track up a sunny slope
covered with sage-scented scrub. Ascend a couple of switchbacks and wonderful views open of Fallen Leaf Lake below
(east), and Lake Tahoe, behind and to the north.

The views improve atop the narrow ridgeback of the
lateral moraine separating Fallen Leaf Lake from Mount
Tallac, with the trail cruising along the spine of the moraine
through Jeffrey pine and mountain hemlock. Drop off the
ridge into a drainage, where the views are replaced by the
shade of pine and fir.

The trail roller-coasters through forest and gully as it
trends north into the shadow of the mountain. Climb up to
and then alongside the creek that issues from Floating Island
Lake. Enter the Desolation Wilderness, then hitch up a final
stretch to the quiet shoreline of the little lake.

The trail skirts the forested south shore of Floating Island
Lake. At the edge of a small talus field just above the tarn, the
trail veers right, resuming the climb via a short staircase composed of blocks of granite. Cross a small meadow and a creek
(stay left on the main trail); beyond, the route traverses a hillside strewn with wildflowers and butterflies in early summer.

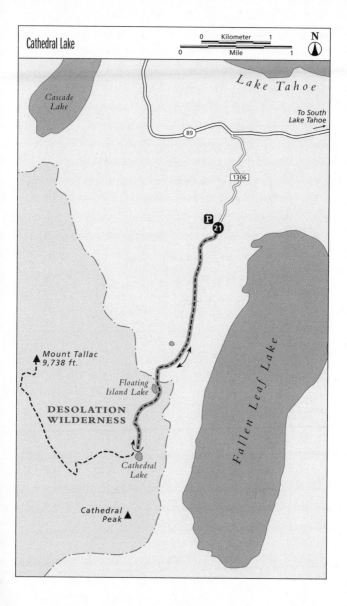

Cathedral Lake

0 Kilometer 1

0 Mile 1

N

Lake Tahoe

Cascade Lake

To South Lake Tahoe

89

1306

P 21

Mount Tallac 9,738 ft.

Floating Island Lake

DESOLATION WILDERNESS

Fallen Leaf Lake

Cathedral Lake

Cathedral Peak

Drop to a second creek crossing, then meander up to a junction with a trail that descends to Fallen Leaf Lake. Stay right (southwest), climbing a last pitch up to Cathedral Lake. Rest and refuel on the rocky shores, then return to the trailhead by the same route.

Miles and Directions

0.0   Start up the trail behind the informational signboard.

0.7   Reach the top of the lateral moraine, and take in views of Fallen Leaf Lake and Lake Tahoe.

1.2   Drop off the moraine.

1.8   Climb along a creek to the Desolation Wilderness boundary.

1.9   Arrive at Floating Island Lake.

2.5   Cross a streamlet and stay right (west) around the talus field.

2.7   Arrive at the signed junction with the trail to Fallen Leaf Lake. Stay right (southwest) and up on the Mount Tallac Trail.

2.8   Reach Cathedral Lake. Rest, then retrace your steps.

5.6   Arrive back at the trailhead.

Options: If you've the will and strength, you can make the steep climb to the summit of Mount Tallac, a hiker's prize about 2.4 miles above and beyond Cathedral Lake.

22 Rainbow Trail

The Taylor Creek Stream Profile Chamber is the main attraction along this charming and popular paved path, but there's more to recommend the Rainbow Trail, including vistas across the marsh surrounding Taylor Creek, bowers of quaking aspen, and comprehensive interpretive signage.

Start: Opposite the Taylor Creek Visitor Center near the Tallac Historic Site, marked with an arch
Distance: 0.6-mile loop
Hiking time: About 45 minutes
Difficulty: Easy
Trail surface: Pavement
Best seasons: Spring, summer, fall
Other trail users: None
Trail amenities: Restrooms, information, water, visitor center
Canine compatibility: Dogs not permitted in the stream chamber or on Kiva Beach, but otherwise allowed on leashes
Fees and permits: None
Schedule: The Taylor Creek Stream Profile Chamber is open Memorial Day to Oct 31 from 8 a.m. until a half hour before the Taylor Creek Visitor Center closes. The Taylor Creek Visitor Center's operating hours vary, but it is generally open from 8 a.m. to 4:30 p.m. daily mid-May to mid-June and during Oct, and from 8 a.m. to 5:30 p.m. daily mid-June through Sept. The trails can be used from sunrise to sunset daily.
Maps: USGS Emerald Bay CA, but a map is not needed.
Trail contact: US Forest Service Lake Tahoe Basin Management Unit, Forest Supervisor's Office, 35 College Dr., South Lake Tahoe, CA 96150; (530) 543-2600; www.fs.usda.gov/ltbmu
Special considerations: The trail is wheelchair accessible.

Finding the trailhead: From the intersection of US 50 and CA 89 in South Lake Tahoe, go northwest on CA 89 for 3.2 miles to the signed turnoff for the Taylor Creek Visitor Center. Turn right (north) onto the visitor center road and follow it to the parking area. GPS: N38 56.133' / W120 03.243'

The Hike

In the clear water behind the glass of the Taylor Creek Stream Profile Chamber, kokanee salmon, their scales lipstick red as they prepare to spawn in autumn, seem to pace in lovesick agitation. They mingle with their cousins: rainbow, brown, and Lahontan cutthroat trout, the latter species native to the deep waters of Lake Tahoe. Larger fish circle lazily in the stream while the smaller dart about swiftly, looking for food or hoping to avoid becoming a meal themselves.

This opportunity to observe life inside a mountain stream from fish-eye level is the highlight of the Rainbow Trail, the experience enhanced by the assistance of a naturalist and information presented on the surrounding interpretive display. But this pleasant walk—easy enough for a toddler to manage—sports many other attractions. The marsh surrounding Taylor Creek is no scenic slouch, resplendent with wildflowers in spring and ringing with birdcall throughout the hiking season. Quaking aspen, turning as vivid a gold as the kokanee's red in fall, provide yet another visual lollipop. The route is lined with interpretive signs and benches, perfect for the entertainment and edification of children of all ages.

The path begins just outside the visitor center, dropping to a marsh overlook and then to a trail junction where the loop begins. Go right (following the arrow), traveling in a counterclockwise direction. Meander through the meadow and skirt the marsh on boardwalks, pausing to take in views toward Lake Tahoe and read the interpretive signs. A bridge spans Taylor Creek, then the trail forks, with one branch leading down and through the stream profile chamber

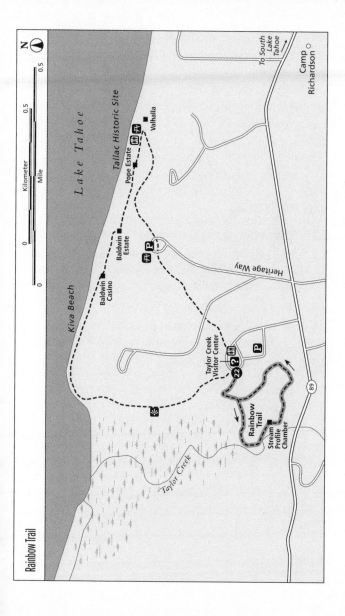

and the other going around. Head down the path into the chamber, view the trout action, then climb back out onto the paved path.

On the far side of the chamber, amid the aspen, pass a "pillow sensor" and rain gauge, along with an interpretive display that explains their functions. Beyond lies an alder spring, and then the tall grasses and wildflowers of the meadow accompany you back to the trail fork. Go right to the visitor center and parking area.

Miles and Directions

0.0   Start on the paved path under the Rainbow Trail arch.

0.1   Visit the marsh overlook, then return to the trail and drop to the start of the loop. Go right (counterclockwise) as indicated by the arrow on the small sign.

0.3   Drop through the stream profile chamber.

0.4   At the Y outside the chamber, go left, past the monitoring station. Close the loop by circling back toward the visitor center.

0.6   Arrive back at the trailhead.

23 Lake of the Sky Trail and Tallac Historic Site

Lake Tahoe's natural history blends with its human history on this pleasant meander, which begins with an exploration of the Taylor Creek Marsh and ends among the spectacular vacation homes of turn-of-the-twentieth-century tycoons.

Start: North side of the Taylor Creek Visitor Center on the Lake of the Sky Trail
Distance: 2.0-mile loop
Hiking time: About 1 hour
Difficulty: Easy
Trail surface: Dirt trail, sand, pavement
Best seasons: Late spring, summer, fall
Other trail users: Maybe a few cyclists and runners
Trail amenities: Restrooms, information, water, visitor center
Canine compatibility: Though leashed dogs are allowed on trails from Valhalla Pier to Tallac Point, Tallac Historic Site is not dog friendly. No dogs are allowed on Kiva Beach.
Fees and permits: None
Schedule: The Taylor Creek Visitor Center's operating hours vary,

but it is generally open from 8 a.m. to 4:30 p.m. daily mid-May to mid-June and during Oct, and from 8 a.m. to 5:30 p.m. daily mid-June through Sept. The trails can be used from sunrise to sunset daily.
Maps: USGS Emerald Bay CA; Lake Tahoe Basin Management Unit Map; National Geographic 803 Lake Tahoe Basin Trail Map; Tom Harrison Recreation Map of Lake Tahoe
Trail contact: US Forest Service Lake Tahoe Basin Management Unit, Forest Supervisor's Office, 35 College Dr., South Lake Tahoe, CA 96150; (530) 543-2600; www.fs.usda.gov/ltbmu
Other: The beach walk from the end of Lake of the Sky Trail to the Tallac Historic Site is not a formal forest service trail.

Finding the trailhead: From the intersection of US 50 and CA 89 in South Lake Tahoe, go northwest on CA 89 for 3.2 miles to the signed turnoff for the Taylor Creek Visitor Center. Turn right (north) onto the visitor center road and follow it to the parking area for the visitor center. GPS: N38 56.165' / W120 03.228'

The Hike

From the Washoe Indians who foraged in the basin to turn-of-the-twentieth-century vacationers who built grand estates and party palaces along the shorelines, Lake Tahoe has been a summertime retreat for thousands of years. This trail loop offers glimpses into what those visitors found here, and what they left behind.

The tour begins on the Lake of the Sky Trail, which heads north from the Taylor Creek Visitor Center, paralleling the Taylor Creek Marsh to Kiva Beach at Tallac Point. The trail is lined with interpretive signs and boasts a viewing deck overlooking the marsh.

At Kiva Beach the formal trail ends, and an informal trail leads east along the beach toward the Tallac Historic Site. Wander down along the waterside for a stretch—if the lake is calm, you'll likely see boats pulling water-skiers and wake-boarders—then hitch up one of the short staircases onto the doubletrack at the interface between forest and beach. Pass the foundations of the Tallac Resort Casino; an interpretive sign describes the ballroom, gambling rooms, bowling alley, and stage that "Lucky" Baldwin built and operated on the site. Baldwin's purchase of the lakefront property in 1880 also resulted in the preservation of the grand old Jeffrey pines that shade picnic areas along the trail.

The path bends right (south) to a gate at the edge of the Tallac Historic Site. Pass through: Once within the site,

Lake of the Sky Trail and Tallac Historic Site

wander at will through the grounds of the impressive Baldwin, Pope, and Heller estates. The exploration can take a few minutes, or the rest of the day. Interpretive signs describe the buildings—cabins, impressive lodges, a museum, a boathouse theater, all with tree-screened lake views—as well as the exhibits preserved at the site. Be sure to visit the wonderful arboretum and garden before you head out to the parking lot to complete the loop. A sign at the north end of the parking area directs you onto a dirt path leading through scrub and woodland back to the visitor center and trailhead.

Miles and Directions

0.0 Begin on the signed, paved Lake of the Sky Trail on the north side of the visitor center. Pass the amphitheater; the trail turns to dirt.

0.2 Visit the viewing platform.

0.4 Reach the end of the Lake of the Sky Trail at Kiva Beach. Turn right (east) and walk along the beach.

0.6 Go right (south) up one of the short staircases onto the trail that parallels the beach. Go left (east) along the wide track past the Baldwin casino.

0.9 The trail bends right (south) to the first buildings of the Tallac Historic Site. Pass into the site, then wander at will.

1.7 Complete your tour in the main parking lot. The signed path back to the Taylor Creek Visitor Center is on the north side of the lot.

1.8 Cross the park road.

2.0 Arrive back at the trailhead.

24 Lam Watah Historic Trail

Follow trail and boardwalk through meadows and stands of Jeffrey pine from Stateline's busy casino district to Lake Tahoe's sprawling Nevada Beach.

Start: Signed trailhead at the junction of US 50 and Kahle Drive
Distance: 2.3 miles out and back
Hiking time: About 1.5 hours
Difficulty: Easy
Trail surface: Decomposed granite, boardwalk, asphalt, sand
Best seasons: Spring, summer, fall
Other trail users: Mountain bikers, trail runners
Trail amenities: Restrooms, information signboards; camping and picnic sites at Nevada Beach

Canine compatibility: Leashed dogs permitted on trail; no dogs allowed on Nevada Beach
Fees and permits: None
Schedule: Sunrise to sunset daily
Maps: USGS South Lake Tahoe (CA, NV); National Geographic 803 Lake Tahoe Basin Trail Map
Trail contact: US Forest Service Lake Tahoe Basin Management Unit, Forest Supervisor's Office, 35 College Dr., South Lake Tahoe, CA 96150; (530) 543-2600; www.fs.usda.gov/ltbmu

Finding the trailhead: The trailhead is just northeast of Stateline's casino district at the corner of US 50 and Kahle Drive. Turn left (north) onto Kahle Drive, then immediately right into the signed parking lot. GPS: N38 58.251' / W119 56.151'

The Hike

Linking the busy casinos of Stateline with Tahoe's shoreline at Nevada Beach, the Lam Watah Historic Trail traverses swatches of meadow and open pine woodland, a wide and gentle walk-and-talk route perfect for a sunset stroll or a short family hike.

Though the route never wanders far from civilization—houses are visible along Kahle Drive at the outset, and the towers of the casinos and the Heavenly Valley gondola rise against the mountain front on the return—the essence of the trail is in the woods and the meadows. Wildflowers light the grasses in spring, and the trees provide shade and a distinctive windblown song played only in the high country. A variety of birds settle in the brush along the willow-bordered stream and pond near the trailhead, and at the end Lake Tahoe spreads northward as far as the eye can see.

The pond is to the right (north) as the trail begins its gentle descent toward the beach. Social trails cut through high desert sages to the waterside and toward homes, but the way forward is obvious. A copse of aspen at the edge of the pond is a bird magnet.

Cross the stream via a curving boardwalk, then enter the first patch of woodland. From here to the beachside campground, the trail drops through meadows and rises through the woods in gentle undulations. Benches along the track offer opportunities for rest and contemplation. In the distance the craggy peaks of Desolation Wilderness cut the horizon.

The route ends at a signed trailhead in the Nevada Beach Campground. To reach the beach, follow the campground road around to the right (north, then southwest) to sandy access trails near the restrooms. Dogs are not allowed on the beach, but it is the perfect place to cool your feet before retracing your steps to the trailhead.

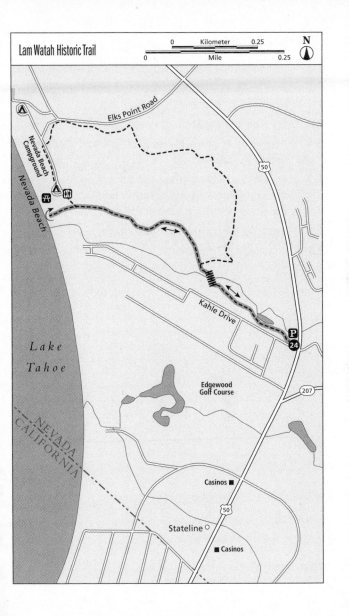

Lam Watah Historic Trail

Kilometer
0   0.25

Mile
0   0.25

N

Elks Point Road

50

Nevada Beach
Campground

Nevada Beach

Kahle Drive

P
24

Lake
Tahoe

Edgewood
Golf Course

207

NEVADA
CALIFORNIA

Casinos

50

Stateline

Casinos

Miles and Directions

0.0 Start by heading down the wide gravel track toward Lake Tahoe.

0.1 Pass the pond. Ignore social trails that break right and left, staying on the main track.

0.3 Cross the boardwalk.

0.4 Trails merge in the woods; remain on the main track heading toward the lakeshore.

1.0 Arrive at the Lam Watah trailhead in the campground. Follow the campground road around to the right (north), then left (southwest) to the sandy beach access by the restrooms.

1.1 Reach the beach, relax for a while, then retrace your steps.

2.3 Arrive back at the trailhead.

25 Castle Rock

A roller-coaster ramble along the Tahoe Rim Trail leads to a towering rock formation perched in the woods, with the lake and its southern rim visible through breaks in the canopy.

Start: North Kingsbury Grade trailhead for the Tahoe Rim Trail
Distance: 3.1-mile loop
Hiking time: 1–2 hours
Difficulty: Moderate
Trail surface: Dirt
Best seasons: Late spring, summer, fall
Other trail users: Mountain bikers, rock climbers
Trail amenities: Restrooms (open seasonally), information signboard
Canine compatibility: Leashed dogs permitted
Fees and permits: None

Schedule: Sunrise to sunset daily
Maps: USGS South Lake Tahoe (CA, NV); Tom Harrison Recreation Map of Lake Tahoe; National Geographic 803 Lake Tahoe Basin Trail Map
Trail contact: US Forest Service Lake Tahoe Basin Management Unit, Forest Supervisor's Office, 35 College Dr., South Lake Tahoe, CA 96150; (530) 543-2600; www.fs.usda.gov/ltbmu. Tahoe Rim Trail Association, 128 Market St., Ste. 3E/PO Box 3267, Stateline, NV 89449; (775) 298-4485; tahoerimtrail.org.

Finding the trailhead: From the junction of US 50 and NV 207 (Kingsbury Grade) in Stateline, drive about 2.5 miles up Kingsbury Grade to the junction with North Benjamin Drive. Turn left (north) onto North Benjamin and follow the main road (it becomes Andria Drive) for 1.8 miles to the end of the pavement in the parking area for the Tahoe Rim Trail and ORV access. GPS: N38 59.770' / W119 53.796'

The Hike

The spires of Castle Rock, a rock climber's destination as well as a hiker's, jut above the treetops not far from the Tahoe Rim Trail (TRT). Round a bend in the spur trail that leads to the crag, and its colorful faces, composed of mottled red, yellow, gray, and brown rock, soar overhead. Unless you brought along your climbing gear, the end of the trail is at the base, where views of Lake Tahoe are filtered through trees. It's a satisfying destination even if you don't make it to the top.

Begin by heading up from the signed TRT trailhead via the access trail, which climbs through open woodland toward the TRT formal. Crest a rise and views open toward Heavenly Valley's ski mountain. A lovely, gentle traverse leads to the junction with the TRT; go left, following the sign indicating the Castle Rock junction lies a mile beyond.

The route begins a gentle descent, with openings in the trees allowing glimpses of the lake and the rim to the south and west. Pass the junction with the Stinger Trail, again staying left on the TRT. The junction with the spur to Castle Rock is at the 1.5-mile mark, just beyond a seasonal stream crossing.

A brief climb leads to a sharp curve with a memorable view past a rock outcrop toward Heavenly. Round the bend and Castle Rock rises above. Climbers' trails break left, toward the steep faces and gullies on the rock's east face; to stay on easy hiking terrain, keep to the right. Climb up and around the shoulder on the north side. The walking route peters out amid slabs facing the lake; find a place to park in the shade on the stones and rest for a while, enjoying the shelter of the pines and the filtered lake views, as well as glimpses of the bony summits of Desolation Wilderness.

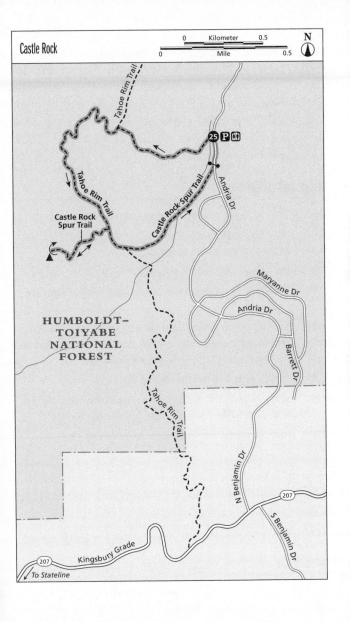

0   Kilometer   0.5

0   Mile   0.5

N

Tahoe Rim Trail

Tahoe Rim Trail

Castle Rock
Spur Trail

Tahoe Rim Trail

Castle Rock Spur Trail

25 P

Andria Dr

Maryanne Dr

Andria Dr

Barrett Dr

HUMBOLDT–
TOIYABE
NATIONAL
FOREST

Tahoe Rim Trail

N Benjamin Dr

S Benjamin Dr

207

Kingsbury Grade

207

To Stateline

To return to the trailhead, retrace your steps to the junction with the TRT and go right. The Castle Rock Trail leading back to the trailhead, marked with a sign, breaks left after a second seasonal stream crossing. The trail widens into a service road as you climb back toward the starting point, with several houses perched on the hillside to the right. The ascent is steady and easy, terminating at a gate at the south end of the trailhead parking area.

Miles and Directions

0.0   Start by heading uphill toward the formal junction with the Tahoe Rim Trail.

0.5   At the junction, go left on the TRT.

1.0   Pass the junction with the Stinger Trail; stay left on the TRT.

1.5   Reach the junction with the spur to Castle Rock. Head right and uphill.

1.8   The trail begins to splinter at the base of Castle Rock. Stay right to circle around on the north side. After you've taken in the views, return to the junction with the TRT.

2.4   At the junction turn right onto the TRT.

2.6   At the junction with the second signed Castle Rock spur trail, turn left onto the spur and begin a gentle climb.

3.1   Pass the gate and arrive back at the trailhead.

26 Angora Lakes

Throw the suits and towels into the day pack and bring the kids: The Angora Lakes Trail is short, sweet, and lovely—the perfect introduction to the pleasures of hiking in the mountains around Lake Tahoe.

Start: Signed trailhead beyond the gate at the south end of the upper parking lot
Distance: 1.0 mile out and back
Hiking time: About 45 minutes
Difficulty: Easy
Trail surface: Dirt access road
Best seasons: Summer, fall
Other trail users: Mountain bikers, the occasional automobile
Trail amenities: Restrooms, fee stations, information sign in the trailhead parking lot; boat rentals, swimming, gifts, food, fresh lemonade at the Angora Lakes Resort
Canine compatibility: Leashed dogs permitted; dogs may not swim in the lake
Fees and permits: Parking fee

Schedule: Hike the trail from sunrise to sunset daily. The resort is open daily from mid-June to mid-Sept.
Maps: USGS Echo Lakes CA, but no map is necessary.
Trail contact: US Forest Service Lake Tahoe Basin Management Unit, Forest Supervisor's Office, 35 College Dr., South Lake Tahoe, CA 96150; (530) 543-2600; www.fs.usda.gov/ltbmu
Other: Angora Lakes Resort offers hikers access to the snack shack (where the lemonade is sold) and kayak and boat rentals. Cabins book well in advance; visit angoralakesresort.com or call (530) 541-2092 for more information.

Finding the trailhead: From the intersection of US 50 and CA 89 in South Lake Tahoe, go northwest on CA 89 for 3 miles to Fallen Leaf Lake Road. Turn left onto Fallen Leaf Lake Road and go 2 miles to Tahoe Mountain Road. Turn left onto Tahoe Mountain Road and follow it for 0.4 mile to FR 1214 (Angora Ridge Road; look for an open gate; the road appears to be dirt at the outset). Turn right onto FR

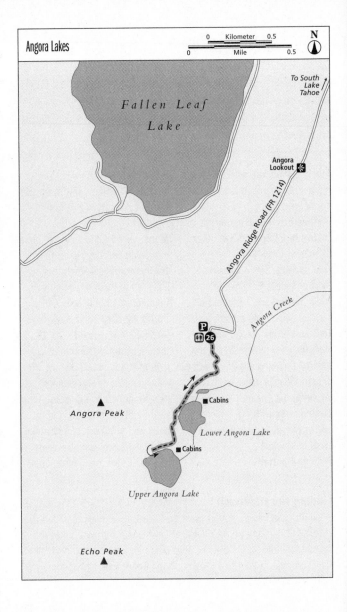

Angora Lakes

0 Kilometer 0.5
0 Mile 0.5

N

Fallen Leaf Lake

To South Lake Tahoe

Angora Lookout

Angora Ridge Road (FR 1214)

Angora Creek

P

26

Angora Peak

Cabins

Lower Angora Lake

Cabins

Upper Angora Lake

Echo Peak

1214 and travel 3 miles on the scenic, narrow, paved roadway to the parking area. GPS: N38 52.261' / W120 03.788'

The Hike

The short romp up to Angora Lakes Resort, with just enough elevation gain to get your heart pumping, lands on the sandy shoreline of Upper Angora Lake. The setting is postcard-perfect, with the blue-green lake pooling in a basin encircled by the stark gray-and-black rock slopes of Echo and Angora Peaks. Trail's end brings cool water for swimming, rowboats for rent, and a snack bar featuring some of the best lemonade money can buy. It's not a wilderness experience, but the short hike leads to one of the South Shore's most desirable family-friendly destinations.

Begin by following the access road up broad arcing turns on a boulder-strewn, forested hillside. After the short climb, the path flattens and is intersected by social paths that lead to private cabins on Lower Angora Lake. Stay on the main track, tracing the west shore of the lower lake.

An exceptionally brief climb leads to the snack bar and cabins on the shores of Upper Angora Lake. The west and south shores are contained by black-streaked terraced cliffs spilling down from Echo and Angora Peaks. The beach hugs the north shore: Stake out a patch of sand, sip some luscious fresh-squeezed lemonade, and enjoy.

Miles and Directions

0.0   Start by heading up the broad, busy dirt track.

0.2   Reach Lower Angora Lake.

0.5   Rest on the shores of Upper Angora Lake, then retrace your steps.

1.0   Arrive back at the trailhead.

27 Glen Alpine

Though the native Washoe were the first to enjoy the waters at what would become known as Glen Alpine Springs Resort, Nathan Gilmore, prospector and cofounder of the Sierra Club, turned the area into an upscale getaway. This easy walk up a forest road partly paved in river cobbles leads to the remnants of the resort.

Start: Gated Glen Alpine trailhead at Lily Lake
Distance: 2.2 miles out and back
Hiking time: About 1.5 hours
Difficulty: Easy
Trail surface: River stone and dirt roadway
Best seasons: Late spring, summer, fall
Other trail users: None
Trail amenities: Parking, restrooms, information signboard, trash cans at the trailhead; information signboards at the Glen Alpine resort site
Canine compatibility: Leashed dogs permitted
Fees and permits: A free wilderness permit, available at the trailhead, is required if you decide to proceed into the Desolation Wilderness, which begins just beyond the Glen Alpine site.

Schedule: 24 hours a day, 7 days a week, year-round
Maps: USGS Emerald Bay CA; Lake Tahoe Basin Management Unit Map; National Geographic 803 Lake Tahoe Basin Trail Map; Tom Harrison Recreation Map of Lake Tahoe
Trail contact: US Forest Service Lake Tahoe Basin Management Unit, Forest Supervisor's Office, 35 College Dr., South Lake Tahoe, CA 96150; (530) 543-2600; www.fs.usda.gov/ltbmu
Special considerations: Parking at the popular Glen Alpine trailhead fills quickly. More parking is available in pullouts along the access road. Fallen Leaf Lake Road is one lane and busy in summer. Travel slowly and be courteous by stopping in wide spots to let oncoming traffic pass safely.

Finding the trailhead: From the intersection of US 50 and CA 89 in South Lake Tahoe, go north on CA 89 for 3 miles to Fallen Leaf Lake Road. Turn left onto Fallen Leaf Lake Road. Pass the turnoff for Angora Lakes at about 2 miles, continuing on Fallen Leaf Lake Road for a total of 5 miles. Pass the lodge and marina, and at the fork just beyond, stay straight, past the fire station, on FR 1216 to Lily Lake. The trailhead parking area is 0.6 mile ahead. GPS: N38 52.627' / W120 04.836'

The Hike

If a hard line could be drawn in the woods, there would be one just above the site of the historic Glen Alpine Springs Resort. Where the gravel road ends and the trail begins, the personality of the backcountry changes abruptly. Below the granite staircase leading into the Desolation Wilderness, remnants of civilization, including a burbling spring and the historic structures of a nineteenth-century resort, huddle on granite slopes among the pines. Step onto the staircase and you pass into the high country, John Muir's "Range of Light" as the naturalist himself may have experienced it back in the day.

The route to Glen Alpine changes with the seasons. In early season or during heavy snow years, the trail may be half submerged in flowing snowmelt. Your boots will get wet, but there's an upside: If the trail past Lily Lake is soggy, the waterfalls spilling down the creek adjacent to the road will be flowing full force.

At the outset the trail/roadway is surfaced in ankle-twisting cobbles. Gates and trail signs keep you on track at forks in the road, though the signs are inconspicuous—brown and mounted above eye level on tree trunks. Parcels

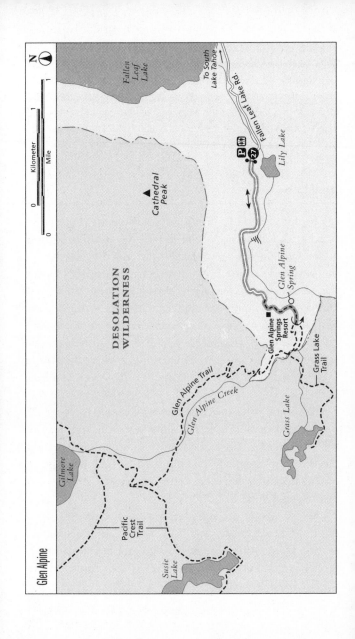

Glen Alpine

To South Lake Tahoe

Fallen Leaf Lake

Fallen Leaf Lake Rd.

Lily Lake

P

27

Cathedral Peak

DESOLATION WILDERNESS

Glen Alpine Spring

Glen Alpine Springs Resort

Grass Lake Trail

Grass Lake

Glen Alpine Trail

Glen Alpine Creek

Gilmore Lake

Pacific Crest Trail

Susie Lake

N

Kilometer

Mile

of private land line this section of the route, with rugged driveways leading to small cabins.

Patches of asphalt are interspersed with the cobbles as you approach a series of cascades on Glen Alpine Creek. Modjeska Falls, at 0.4 mile, is about 75 feet in height. The display is best (and loudest) in June and early July. Past the falls the trail climbs to another driveway intersection; go left (west), following the trail sign.

Continue past several more cabins, traveling through a lovely mixed evergreen forest with a lush understory of wild berries and flowers that bloom in spring, and deciduous trees and shrubs that turn yellow and orange in fall. The cabins have all of Desolation Wilderness as a backyard.

Just beyond an old barn, a trail sign points you to the right (west) and into what is left of the Glen Alpine Springs Resort, which operated for the better part of a century. Take a break and check out the ruins of the once-thriving enterprise, including the soda spring, which still burbles and pops. Interpretive signs thoroughly describe the history of the resort, and a map directs you to the different structures that were part of the complex. After you've finished your exploration, return as you came.

Miles and Directions

0.0   Start by passing the green gate at the trailhead and walking up the cobbled roadway.

0.3   Cross a stream (dry in late season) and pass a gate and trail sign.

0.4   At the junction with a private access road, stay right and follow the "Trails" sign. Check out the falls before continuing up the river-stone roadway.

0.5 At a second junction with a private drive, stay left, again following the "Trails" sign.

1.1 Pass the old barn and enter the Glen Alpine Springs Resort. Explore the site, then return as you came.

2.2 Arrive back at the trailhead.

Options: A number of enticing destinations lie above the Glen Alpine resort site in the Desolation Wilderness. With two lakes, two waterfalls, and three creek crossings, the hike to Grass Lake is invigorating if not exactly easy. The junction with the trail leading to the little lake is 1.8 miles from the trailhead (0.7 mile past Glen Alpine). You'll have to negotiate a triplet of creek crossings to reach the lake basin, which could be tricky in early season when runoff is at its height. The lake is at 2.5 miles, cupped in a glacial basin with a seasonal waterfall spilling down the opposite cliff in early season.

If you continue on the Glen Alpine Trail past the Grass Lake turnoff, you will climb deeper into Desolation. Gilmore Lake lies 4.3 miles from the trailhead, in a shallow bowl on the slopes of Mount Tallac. And Tallac itself is a goal, albeit out of the easy range, with the summit at more than 9,700 feet. Other destinations include Susie Lake, Half Moon Lake, and Lake Aloha, each worthy of an overnight trip as much as an arduous day hike.

28 Pacific Crest Trail at Echo Lakes

This leg of the famous Pacific Crest Trail stretches from the exposed granite slabs that border Lower Echo Lake to the forested shore of Upper Echo Lake. The hiking is easy, and the views arc north into the craggy silver heights of the Desolation Wilderness.

Start: Signed Pacific Crest Trail (PCT)/Tahoe Rim Trail (TRT) trailhead on the far side of the dam behind Echo Chalet

Distance: 2.5 miles one way (with a boat taxi shuttle) or 5.0 miles out and back

Hiking time: 1–2 hours one-way or 3–4 hours out and back

Difficulty: Moderate due to trail length and rocky terrain

Trail surface: Dirt and rock singletrack

Best seasons: Summer, fall

Other trail users: None

Trail amenities: Food, lodging, restrooms, and information are available at the trailhead. A dock and direct telephone line to the boat taxi are at the Upper Echo Lake endpoint; there is also a credit card–only pay phone.

Canine compatibility: Leashed dogs permitted

Fees and permits: There is no fee if you hike out and back; a fee is charged for the on-demand boat taxi. You must fill out a free permit, available at the trailhead, if you plan to hike into the Desolation Wilderness.

Schedule: The trail can be hiked sunrise to sunset daily. Boat taxis are available until 5:30 p.m. in the summer months.

Maps: USGS Echo Lakes CA; National Geographic 803 Lake Tahoe Basin Trail Map; Tom Harrison Recreation Map of Lake Tahoe

Trail contact: US Forest Service Lake Tahoe Basin Management Unit, Forest Supervisor's Office, 35 College Dr., South Lake Tahoe, CA 96150; (530) 543-2600; www.fs.usda.gov/ltbmu. Tahoe Rim Trail Association, 128 Market St., Ste. 3E/PO Box 3267, Stateline, NV 89449; (775) 298-4485; tahoerimtrail.org

Finding the trailhead: From the junction of US 50 and CA 89 in South Lake Tahoe, drive west on US 50 for 10 miles, over Echo Summit, to a right (north) turn onto Johnson Pass Road (with sign). Go 0.5 mile on Johnson Pass Road to Echo Lakes Road. Turn left (north) onto Echo Lakes Road and drive 1.2 miles to the Echo Chalet. Parking can be tight; if no parking is available at the chalet, scout a spot along the road or in the upper parking lot and walk the short distance down to the chalet and trailhead. Contact the forest service for latest parking options and restrictions. GPS: N38 50.085' / W120 02.611'

The Hike

The granite basin that holds the Echo Lakes, at the edge of the Desolation Wilderness and near the crest of the Sierra, provides a lovely setting for this stretch of the combined Pacific Crest and Tahoe Rim Trails. The lower lake is larger, and the route is exposed to the sun and wind, with the granite base of Flagpole Peak underlying the treadway. To the north the broad pass between Keiths Dome (on the northwest side) and Ralston Peak (on the southwest side) forms a headwall of great silvery terraces, a beckoning and imposing gateway into the wilderness beyond. The upper lake, by contrast, is screened from hikers' view by a dense pine and fir forest; the trail here is enveloped in peaceful green.

The hike begins at the southern end of the lower lake near the Echo Chalet. Cross the causeway atop the dam and the bridge that spans the spillway. The trail switches uphill past trail signs to a trail intersection; head left (north) on the Pacific Crest Trail, climbing up through manzanita onto granite slabs. The trail is etched in the bleached granite, a narrow but well-traveled traverse that stays about 200 feet above the surface of the navy-blue water.

Pacific Crest Trail at Echo Lakes

N

To South Lake Tahoe

Echo Lakes Road

Echo Chalet

28
?
P

50

Johnson Pass Road

50

Kilometer

Mile

0   1

0   1

▲ Flagpole Peak

Lower Echo Lake

Cabins

Cabins

Cabins

Cabins

Upper Echo Lake

Cabins

Telephone

To Desolation Wilderness

The first of many charming vacation cabins sits not far beyond a section of trail augmented with asphalt. Gentle climbing leads to a trail sign near some of those cabins, then two switchbacks navigate the steepest part of the hike. The ascent moderates as you approach the far reaches of the lower lake.

Drop through a rocky, brushy section in the shadow of an overhanging slab streaked with black, gray, and orange, then climb through the gap between the two lakes, where the trail and bordering hillside are stained orange with iron that has oxidized in the rock. Brief views of the upper lake and stony islands in the narrow passage connecting the blue tarns are visible.

The traverse along the wooded shores of the upper lake is easy, and the forest shades a colorful understory of brush and wildflowers ringing with birdcall. Crest a small rise and, as you begin to head downhill, look for the "Taxi" sign nailed to a big fir tree. The narrow path to the boat dock branches off to the left. Drop about 50 yards to the dock, which is the turnaround point. You can either take a break overlooking the upper lake, then hike back as you came, or pick up the phone and call for the boat taxi. I recommend the taxi: The ride is a treat.

Miles and Directions

0.0   Start by crossing the dam at the south end of Lower Echo Lake. At the TRT/PCT signs and map, head up and right, then around left to parallel the lakeshore.

0.3   Climb across a granite slab.

1.1   Pass a trail sign above a cluster of cabins. The trail switchbacks up the hillside.

1.6	Pass a black-streaked overhanging rock on the right, then the trail flattens alongside cabins.
2.0	Cross the red soils of the isthmus separating the upper and lower lakes.
2.3	Pass through open woodland.
2.5	At the "Taxi" sign nailed to a tree, turn left and drop to the boat dock. This is the turnaround point for an out-and-back hike or the place to call for the boat taxi.
5.0	Arrive back at the trailhead.

Options: The PCT and TRT continue into the Desolation Wilderness, a high-country wonderland of lakes. The wilderness is a backpacker's paradise; you can do a long loop, then return to Upper Echo Lake to take a boat taxi back to your car.

29 Big Meadow

A quick climb along a churning creek leads to the seductive expanse of Big Meadow, alive with wildflowers that rotate with the seasons. The waterway becomes a meander among the grasses, where you are likely to find yourself alone with its chatter and the wind rustling the pines.

Start: Lower parking lot at the Big Meadow trailhead on CA 89

Distance: 2.0 miles out and back

Hiking time: About 1 hour

Difficulty: Easy

Trail surface: Dirt singletrack

Best seasons: Late spring, summer, fall

Other trail users: Mountain bikers, equestrians

Trail amenities: Restrooms, trash cans, information signboard with map at the trailhead

Canine compatibility: Leashed dogs permitted

Fees and permits: None

Schedule: Sunrise to sunset daily

Maps: USGS Freel Peak and Echo Lake CA; National Geographic 803 Lake Tahoe Basin Trail Map; Tahoe Rim Trail map available at the trailhead

Trail contact: US Forest Service Lake Tahoe Basin Management Unit, Forest Supervisor's Office, 35 College Dr., South Lake Tahoe, CA 96150; (530) 543-2600; www.fs.usda.gov/ltbmu. Tahoe Rim Trail Association, 128 Market St., Ste. 3E/PO Box 3267, Stateline, NV 89449; (775) 298-4485; tahoerimtrail.org.

Finding the trailhead: From the intersection of US 50 and CA 89 in South Lake Tahoe, drive west on US 50/CA 89 for 4.7 miles to Meyers, where the two highways diverge. Turn left (southeast) onto CA 89 and go 5.1 miles to the signed Big Meadow trailhead on the left (north). The signed trailhead is in the lower parking lot. GPS: N38 47.316' / W120 00.044'

The Hike

Mountain meadows witness the passage of the seasons in magical ways. In springtime and early summer, wildflowers erupt in sheets of red, purple, pink, orange, blue, white, and yellow, and the grasses vibrate with butterflies and bees harvesting nectar. By late summer and autumn, the flowers have faded, but the grasses have absorbed the warm hues of the summer sun, glistening gold and rattling in the breezes. Even in winter, blanketed in thick snow, a mountain meadow is meditative and impressive.

Big Meadow is perfect in all these incarnations.

To reach the meadow, begin in the lower trailhead parking area, just beyond the information sign. Pass a blue-and-white sign for the Tahoe Rim Trail almost immediately; the trail runs alongside CA 89 until it climbs to the edge of the asphalt and crosses the road.

The path steepens on the other side of the highway, ascending through a forest of mixed evergreens. Climb a log-and-granite staircase, which undoubtedly confounds mountain bikers navigating the route. Highway noise filters through the forest, but the rumbling of Big Meadow Creek helps mask the sound.

The trail flattens as the highway noises fade; the boulder-strewn woodland instead harbors birdsong and windsong. At the trail fork, go right (south), following the arrow that points to Meiss Meadow (aka Big Meadow); the left-hand trail leads to Scotts Lake.

Traverse a brief, final stretch of woodland, then the meadow opens. The path, worn into the turf, leads to a footbridge across the clear creek, then cuts a straight line through the grasses and wildflowers to the dense forest that buffers

Big Meadow

0   Kilometer   0.25
0   Mile   0.25

N

89

29

← To South
Lake Tahoe

Tahoe Rim Trail

Big
Meadow

Big Meadow Creek

To Scotts
Lake →

the southern edge of the grassland and carpets the rolling mountains that cradle it.

The turnaround point is at the interface of the meadow and forest, though you can continue into the woodland. Sun-bleached stumps, once sturdy enough to provide restful seats and now cracked and rotting, mark the spot. Return as you came.

Miles and Directions

0.0   Start at the signed trailhead.

0.1   Cross CA 89.

0.6   At the trail intersection stay right (south) on the signed "Meiss Meadow" (aka Big Meadow) trail.

0.7   Reach the edge of the meadow.

1.0   Arrive at the turnaround point at the southwest edge of the meadow. Take a breather, then retrace your steps.

2.0   Arrive back at the parking lot.

Option: Though it lies outside the Lake Tahoe basin proper, if you are traveling farther south on CA 89, consider hiking the Winnemucca and Round Top Lakes Loop in the Mokelumne Wilderness. The wildflower bloom on the slopes below Winnemucca Lake is unsurpassed. The setting of Round Top Lake, below a dark sawtooth ridgeline punctuated with permanent snowfields, is picture-book perfect. The trail blends challenge with reward splendidly. Technically a lollipop, the route is 5.3 miles in length, and moderately difficult. To reach the trailhead at Woods Lake Campground, follow CA 89 from Meyers to its junction with CA 88, and continue over Carson Pass on CA 88 toward the Kirkwood ski resort to the Woods Lake Campground turnoff. GPS: N38 41.493' / W120 00.573'

About the Author

Tracy Salcedo has written more than twenty FalconGuides to destinations in California and Colorado, including *Hiking Waterfalls in Northern California*, *Hiking Lassen Volcanic National Park*, *Hiking Through History San Francisco*, *Best Hikes Sacramento*, and Best Easy Day Hikes guides to the San Francisco Bay Area, Reno, Sacramento, Fresno, Boulder, Denver, and Aspen. She is also the author of *Historic Yosemite National Park*, *Historic Denali National Park and Preserve*, and *Death in Mount Rainier National Park*. Visit laughingwaterink.com for more.